CLEARLY CHRISTIAN

Following Jesus in This Age of Confusion

A. Trevor Sutton

CONCORDIA PUBLISHING HOUSE · SAINT LOUIS

PRAISE FOR *CLEARLY CHRISTIAN*

Trevor Sutton is one of my favorite authors for anything where culture and Christianity meet. *Clearly Christian* does not disappoint! Sutton utilizes a timeline of history, engaging discussion questions, biblical study, and witty humor to guide readers from the chaos of our world into a solid understanding of the value and presence of the Gospel in the midst of the challenges of our current cultural context. Sutton's wellspring of knowledge is made relevant page after page. At the end of the day, when readers set this book down, they will still hear the echoes of the author's deep desire that they might walk away with the fullness of God's Gospel grace for each of them.

—DEACONESS HEIDI GOEHMANN, LCSW, LIMPH
AUTHOR AND ADVOCATE AT ILOVEMYSHEPHERD.COM

Though the world has access to more information than ever before, it is also more confused than it ever has been. People are seeking answers to their confusion, but often they look everywhere but the church and to everyone but Christians for answers. Christianity has been defined and redefined by our culture and is often seen as irrelevant, judgmental, and uninspiring. Sutton does a masterful job of reminding us that, as much as everything continues to change, the simple message of God's grace through Jesus remains unchanged and is as relevant and needed as ever. *Clearly Christian* will humble you, challenge you, and inspire you to boldly live as a follower of Jesus in a lost and confused world.

—REV. TIM NIEKERK
SENIOR PASTOR
SALEM LUTHERAN CHURCH, TOMBALL, TX

Trevor Sutton offers approachable theological insight to the weary Christian who's overrun by today's dizzying pace of information. His advice for navigating social media as Christians is poignant and practical, and it should be required reading before we log on to social media. He's absolutely right: we need more Jesus. Sutton remains one of the most accessible theologians. I'll be returning to this book again and again to be refreshed by its truth and clarity in helping Christians understand and respond to confusing claims surrounding the faith.

—SETH HINZ
ASSISTANT TO THE PRESIDENT—WEB/MEDIA DIRECTOR
MICHIGAN DISTRICT, LCMS

Twenty-first-century Christians need to know, defend, share, and practice their faith with authenticity and integrity. *Clearly Christian* weaves all four of these efforts together in one book. Sutton skillfully names contemporary faith challenges, answers these challenges, and equips readers to take simple, meaningful, faithful action to meet these challenges.

—REV. AARON PERRY, PHD
ASSISTANT PROFESSOR OF PASTORAL THEOLOGY AND LEADERSHIP
WESLEY SEMINARY, MARION, IN

Counteracting a cliché-ridden culture and church, Trevor Sutton brings the disarming truth of the Christian faith into bold relief. Using historical insight, scholarly analysis, and practical conversation, *Clearly Christian* provides a counterpoint to confused pious platitudes and reveals the refreshing goodness of God's grace for the world.

—REV. MICHAEL W. NEWMAN
PRESIDENT, TEXAS DISTRICT, LCMS
AUTHOR OF *HOPE WHEN YOUR HEART BREAKS: NAVIGATING GRIEF AND LOSS*

To Dave Davis and Zerit Yohannes,
who constantly teach me what it means
to be clearly Christian.

Published by Concordia Publishing House
3558 S. Jefferson Avenue, St. Louis, MO 63118-3968
1-800-325-3040 • cph.org

Manufactured in the United States of America

Library of Congress Cataloging-in-Publication Data

Names: Sutton, A. Trevor, author.

Title: Clearly Christian : following Jesus in this age of confusion / A Trevor Sutton.

Description: St. Louis : Concordia Publishing House, 2018.

Identifiers: LCCN 2018029928 (print) | LCCN 2018034460 (ebook) | ISBN

9780758657183 | ISBN 9780758657176

Subjects: LCSH: Christianity. | Common fallacies.

Classification: LCC BR121.3 (ebook) | LCC BR121.3 .S88 2018 (print) | DDC 230--dc23

LC record available at https://lccn.loc.gov/2018029928

1   2   3   4   5   6   7   8   9   10   27   26   25   24   23   22   21   20   19   18

TABLE OF CONTENTS

ACKNOWLEDGMENTS

Some books are easier to write than others. This was not one of those books. I found this to be an incredibly challenging project. And I think I know the reason why: we live in an age of confusion. (Mis)information swells and swirls all around us. Time speeds faster and faster every single day. Digital distractions are our constant companions. And confusion permeates our daily life. Trying to write a book about clear Christianity while living in a world of confusion was a challenging endeavor.

I am grateful for the help and support of many people through the process of writing this book. As always, I would like to thank my wife, Elizabeth, for her endless patience and support. I am deeply thankful for my daughters, Grace and Hannah, and for their love and prayers for me while writing this book. I am also appreciative of the many times in which they forced me to take a break from writing in order to have a greatly needed dance party in the living room of our home.

God has used many people in my life to help me understand more clearly what it means to follow Jesus. I am deeply indebted to my parents, Mark and Jane, and my siblings, Ashleigh and Connor, for teaching me the faith. I am tremendously thankful to God for my congregation, St. Luke Lutheran Church (Meridian Township and Lansing, Michigan), and their continual support and encouragement. And God has used many, many others not listed here to sharpen my understanding, untangle my confusion, and clarify my confession of Jesus.

Lastly, I would like to thank Laura Lane, Alexa Hatesohl, and the rest of the team at Concordia Publishing House for their guidance and editorial wisdom. This book would never have happened without their patience, wisdom, support, and encouragement.

To God be the glory!

INTRODUCTION

IKEA is known around the world for self-assembly furniture. One of the ways the company offers customers modern design at a reasonable price is by having consumers assemble the furniture themselves. And since IKEA sells their products all around the world, the instruction manuals have little to no text that would require extensive translating for use in different countries. Instead, the assembly instructions are conveyed entirely by pictures.

Taking a box of random pieces—bolts and screws, boards and handles, knobs and dowels—and trying to put it all together to make a desk, while being guided only by pictures, is no small feat. Assembling IKEA furniture requires an investment of blood, sweat, tears, and time. Some professional counselors apparently even prescribe assembling this furniture as part of couple's therapy. The thought is, if a couple can put together a piece of furniture without killing each other, then they can put together a marriage without killing each other.

If you have ever assembled this furniture, then you are undoubtedly familiar with the iconic IKEA man. He is the cartoon figure used in the assembly manual pictures. He is depicted in various ways in the instructions: opening boxes, reading the manual, getting help from a friend, and so forth. However, if you ask me, the best depiction of the IKEA man is the one that has him staring at a pile of random pieces with a question mark next to his head.

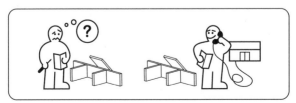

He is looking at the pieces and the instruction manual while wondering where he went wrong with his life. The next picture shows the man calling for help to understand how to assemble all the parts and pieces.

> **The point is this:** If you are confused, then you should get some clarification. If you are unclear as to how all the parts and pieces fit together, then you should get a clearer understanding.

This book will do exactly that for you. (To be absolutely clear, it will not help you assemble IKEA furniture; you are on your own for that.) Instead, this book will provide clarification in the midst of confusion about what it means to be a follower of Jesus. This book addresses many common misconceptions surrounding the Christian faith. The pages that follow work hard to untangle the misinformation from the information and separate falsehood from truth. The layers of misinformation clouding clear Christianity are pervasive in our culture. And there is not just one layer of misunderstanding; there are layers upon layers upon layers of misunderstanding. This book attempts to peel away the resin obscuring the Christian faith. Just as sandpaper grinds away layers of old varnish, this book aims to grind away the layers of errors. By the end, you will have a clearer confession of your faith, hope, and trust in Christ Jesus. And those who do not know Jesus—or what it means to follow Him—will have a clearer knowledge of what it means to be a Christian.

WHAT TO EXPECT

It will be helpful to have some guidance about what to expect from this book. The pages that follow will weave together some disparate and seemingly disconnected topics. At times, you may think it is a stretch to connect ancient history, the internet, and the Christian faith. It may seem far-fetched to draw parallels between the earliest confusion depicted in Genesis and the present-day confusion that is rampant on social media. Let me encourage you to read the whole book, engage all the arguments, and consider all the examples. My hope is that by the end you will agree, "What has been is what will be, and what has been done is what will be done, and there is nothing new under the sun" (Ecclesiastes 1:9). You can expect the following in this book:

Expect Jesus: Clear Christianity is about Jesus. He is not merely a part of Christianity. Jesus is the core of Christianity. If you take Jesus out of Christianity, it ceases to be Christianity. Jesus is not part of a pantheon with Moses, Paul, and Mother Teresa. He is not a model of perfect morality that Christians now must follow. He is God in human flesh, King of all creation, and Savior of the nations. He was crucified for our sins, placed dead in the tomb, and raised to new life. Therefore, He is Lord. He makes all things new, delivers the forgiveness of sins, and reconciles us to God. There is no Christianity apart from Jesus. You can expect Jesus in this book.

Expect Culture: This is a very, very difficult word to define. Smarter people have tried and failed to come up with an adequate and comprehensive definition of this word. Knowing my own limitations, I will not even try to offer a comprehensive definition for culture. For our purposes, suffice to say that culture is the characteristic features of daily existence shared by people in a particular place and time. These include the social practices, attitudes, and beliefs of a group of people. Another word for this is *zeitgeist* (the spirit of the age).

The trouble is this: people are not all the same. There will always be people living and functioning in ways that are distinct from the majority of people around them. To be sure, there is no such thing as a single, monolithic culture in any one time or place. However, it is possible to make broad observations and generalizations about a culture. Schools, universities, companies, congregations, and organizations have particular cultures; these groups have unique ways of thinking, speaking, acting, and interacting with others. On a far greater scale, an entire community or country has a culture. This book discusses modern culture and society in a broad way. You can expect this book to talk about contemporary culture, internet culture, and the spirit of our age at this present time.

Expect Technology, Internet, and Social Media: This book explores the topic of technology and how it influences our lives. It is important to know that technology is not limited to hover boards and ray guns; technology is not narrowly defined as new stuff or modern inventions. Instead, technology has to do with making, producing, or crafting something. In this regard, technology encompasses many diverse objects: computers, cars, books, roads, bridges, smartphones, and many other objects that have been made or produced. This book explores how technology influences our world generally and the Christian faith specifically.

You can also expect a lot of discussion about the internet and social media in this book. Few things are more ubiquitous in modern life than these digital technologies. There is a staggering number of people around the world who use the internet on a daily basis. The number of people—even in impoverished and developing countries—on social media platforms is also dizzying. The world has been profoundly changed by the internet and social media. This book aims to address the many ways in which the internet and social media have affected the Christian faith.

Expect Theology and Church History: Finally, you can expect theology and Church history in this book. Before you nod off to sleep upon hearing those words, let me explain. There is no reason why either theology or Church history must be boring, dusty, or narcolepsy-inducing. Yes, there are many words and terms that may be unfamiliar to you. Yes, the names and events are from another time and place. Nevertheless, these are tremendously important matters. The people of Jesus—not only pastors, but all the people of Jesus—should lean in and learn theology. Why? Because it is the study of God, God's Word, and God's work in the world through Christ Jesus. Those are some pretty universally important topics. Same thing goes for Church history; it explores the life and thought of the people of God through the generations and how this influences the Church today. This book addresses these topics in an accessible and engaging way.

BOOK OVERVIEW

This book is divided into two sections. It will be helpful to know ahead of time what these sections are and why the book is organized in this way.

PART 1: THE AGE OF CONFUSION

The first part of the book gives a broad description of and context for how our world has descended into such profound and widespread confusion. Drawing on Scripture and history, this section explores what it means to be confused about God, how this confusion has been manifested throughout human history, and how it has spread over the generations up until the present day. This section also focuses on how the internet and social media have amplified the confusion in our world. You can think of this section as describing the seed and soil of confusion that have produced the harvest of confusion described in the second section of the book.

PART 2: CLEARING THE CONFUSION

The second part of the book goes into far greater detail than the first part. After looking at the historical origins of our confusion, the second part of the book looks at specific ways that people are currently confused about Christianity. This part of the book addresses common misconceptions and accusations made against the followers of Jesus. You have undoubtedly heard claims like these before:

> Being a Christian is about being a good person, rejecting the physical world, following old-fashioned traditions, judging others, checking your brain at the front door of the church, finding happiness, being overly political, and winning arguments. If you want to be part of that community, then you must subscribe to those tenets.

The chapters in this section of the book clarify the confusion bound up in these claims and offer a clear confession of the Christian faith.

Clear > Confusion =

Each chapter in the second part of the book ends with a brief discussion of how the people of Jesus can prioritize clear Christianity over confusion. These Clear > Confusion mini-sections intend to give you practical and realistic ways to embody the chapters in daily life. In other words, the goal is that you take what you have learned in reading the chapters and actually do something about it in your school, office, neighborhood, or social networks.

SPOILER ALERT

One final note before you read this book. *It does not cover the entire depth and breadth of the Christian faith.* You will certainly read through this book and say, "Hey! What about _____?" And I will say, "Yes, you are totally correct." This book is not intended to be a comprehensive discussion of everything that constitutes the Christian faith. It is not intended to be a dogmatics textbook that explores all the core topics of theology. Rather, this book addresses some of the most commonly misunderstood and confused aspects of the Christian faith.

Clear Christianity is something that the world desperately needs. In a world of counterfeits, the Christian faith is real, solid, and substantive. The Holy Spirit convicts us of our sins and shortcomings and leads us to real repentance. God leads us to be open and honest about the fact that we are poor, miserable sinners in need of a Savior. The followers of Jesus do not hide behind superficial smiles, fake fronts, and flimsy facades. Instead, clear Christianity confesses something real: Real promises. Real grace. Real forgiveness. And real life in Jesus!

THE AGE OF CONFUSION

Part 1

1

A BRIEF HISTORY OF CONFUSION

Confusion. If we could use just one word to capture the essence of modern life, then this would be it. Life in the twenty-first century is a cornucopia of confusion. We have an excess of many things—gadgets, technology, information, cat memes, globalization—but nothing is more abundant than confusion.

Perhaps you disagree. How does this one word exemplify all of modern life? There must be other words that do a better job of capturing the zeitgeist of our times. What about *progress? networked? globalized? technological? tolerant? post-postmodern?*

All these words do describe modern life in some way, shape, or form. Nevertheless, each of them is riddled with confusion. Progress seemingly moves us ever forward, yet it feels a lot like we are going backward. Networks can connect us to people around the globe, yet we have a hard time remembering the name of our next-door neighbor. Globalization makes the world an increasingly smaller place, yet the divisiveness of racism and violence constantly push us apart. Technology makes life easier yet infinitely more complicated. Tolerance does help us strive to understand one another better, but tolerance for anything and everything has also turned society into a feckless blob of opinions. Postmodernity is becoming post-postmodernity, which will eventually become post-post-postmodernity.

Let's just admit we are confused.

Ironically, the Information Age has turned into the Age of Confusion. We have access to more knowledge than any generation that has ever lived. The internet connects our fingers and brains and eyes to a worldwide web of information. The invisible gossamer threads of this web of information join together with other threads at an incredible speed. A simple search of the internet results in millions of possibilities and terabytes of data. We have more information on our smartphones alone than the ancient Library of Alexandria in Egypt. And yet, we also have more misinformation and confusion than ever before.

Daily life in our brave new world requires hacking through a jungle of opinions, navigating an uncharted ocean of misinformation, and climbing above the fog of rumors in order to reach the summit of truth. This is no easy task.

WHEN DID THIS CONFUSION BEGIN?

Like many English words, the word *confuse* comes to us by way of Latin. It has its origins in the Latin word *confundo*. The Latin word has the sense of pouring together or mixing two different substances. Confusion is the mingling and mixing of truth and falsehood, information and misinformation, knowledge and ignorance. Like ink poured into water, confusion is falsehood poured into truth resulting in an opaque mess. Even just a drop of ink mingled with clear water results in a completely unclear mixture.

To be certain, confusion is not a new phenomenon. Though we may currently be experiencing its zenith, the Age of Confusion originated long ago. When did confusion first begin? Was it when Adam was naming the animals and he first encountered the aardvark? Or perhaps confusion became part of the human experience when Adam awoke from a deep slumber and sensed that his rib cage felt different? Although aardvarks and missing ribs are befuddling, neither of these count as confusion in the precise sense of the term. Instead, the first instance of confusion occurred when the serpent said, "Did God actually say, 'You shall not eat of any tree in the garden'?" (Genesis 3:1). This may not readily appear to be confusion. (At least not in the way we often think of confusion.) Nevertheless, this is the moment when confusion first jammed open a door into this world.

Notice the subtlety of this confusion. God had spoken a clear word to His human creatures:

> And the LORD God commanded the man, saying, "You may surely eat of every tree of the garden, but of the tree of the knowledge of good and evil you shall not eat, for in the day that you eat of it you shall surely die." (Genesis 2:16–17)

These words were easily understood. And yet, they were confused by just one word. Did God *really* say that? Are you *sure* you heard Him correctly? What if His Word was not *entirely* true? Just a drop of inky confusion. Just a word of falsehood. Just a tiny bit of obfuscation. And it spread and spread.

Confusion, just like sin, is not of God. It is a deviation away from God. Mingling truth and falsehood is an aberration of God's perfect plan for creation. The apostle Paul makes this clear when he says, "For God is not a God of confusion but of peace" (1 Corinthians 14:33). God is not the author of confusion, nor does He desire confusion. On the contrary, God is the author of truth and clarity, peace and wholeness.

Metastasizing like a cancer, confusion spread from the serpent's words into all creation. Sin confused how Adam and Eve related to God: "And he [Adam] said, 'I heard the sound of You in the garden, and I was afraid, because I was naked, and I hid myself'" (Genesis 3:10). Sin confused how husband and wife related to each other (Genesis 3:7, 12). Sin confused the relationships within the family (Genesis 4:8–9). The pathology of this disease was not confined to ancient history or a single generation. Sin confused human hearts and minds, communities, and all the earth (Genesis 6:5). A drop of ink in water spreads throughout the entire glass; a drop of sin spreads confusion throughout all of God's creation.

THE DEATH SENTENCE FOR CONFUSION
– THE LIFE OF JESUS –

God still provided clarity, even in the midst of this confusion. He spoke clear words of promise to Abraham (Genesis 12:1–3). He made His power clear to Israel through the Passover and deliverance from Egypt (Exodus 12). He made His presence clearly known through their wilderness wanderings and entrance into the Promised Land (Exodus 16:10; Deuteronomy 31:3–6). He made His Word clearly heard through the prophets (Isaiah 43; Jeremiah 29:10–14). He made His promise of a Savior clear to all generations (Genesis 3:15; Isaiah 53; Jeremiah 31:31–34). God made it clear that when He sent His Son He would penetrate the inky confusion of sin with truth and clarity, love and mercy, justice and power: "The people who walked in darkness have seen a great light; those who dwelt in a land of deep darkness, on them has light shone" (Isaiah 9:2).

Jesus is clarity overcoming confusion. He is light shining in the darkness, peace quelling chaos, truth speaking over the noise of falsehood. God came into our confusion and brought clarity. Jesus proclaimed the Word of God with power and authority. Jesus brought ease to diseased people, rest to restless hearts, and life to lifeless bodies. Jesus came into a world of confusion, falsehood, and darkness to bring clarity, truth, and light: "I am the light of the world. Whoever follows Me will not walk in darkness, but will have the light of life" (John 8:12).

There is no confusion in the Gospel of Jesus Christ. No mingling of truth and falsehood, information and misinformation, Good News and bad news. The Gospel speaks truly Good News: Jesus' life, death, and resurrection have made all things new. His resurrection was not fake news. Hundreds of witnesses used their eyes, hands, and minds to confirm the resurrection of Jesus. And this Good News is not some abstract concept; it is the Good News that Jesus is for you. The truth and power of the Gospel has put death to death. The thick confusion of sin has been scattered on the cross. The penetrating clarity of new life has emerged from the tomb. Truth lives because Jesus has driven a nail through the very heart of falsehood.

Confusion is dead; Jesus is alive.

THE EARLY CHURCH
– SENT INTO THE CONFUSION –

Jesus opposed confusion by speaking clear truth with authority. He cleared the confusion within minds and hearts by teaching God's Word to large crowds and small groups of disciples and through one-on-one conversations. However, Jesus also had another strategy for clearing the confusion in this world: the Church. Jesus authoritatively sent the Church to proclaim clear truth in a world of confusion: "And He appointed twelve (whom He also named apostles) so that they might be with Him and He might send them out to preach" (Mark 3:14). The word *apostle* means "one who has been sent." On a number of occasions during His earthly ministry, Jesus authoritatively sent His disciples (Mark 6:7; Luke 10:1–20; Matthew 28:16–20).

After Jesus' resurrection and ascension, the Christians in the Early Church set about the work Jesus sent them to do—clearly confessing the Gospel within a world of confusion. On Pentecost, the Holy Spirit came just as Jesus had promised (Acts 2). And people were confused. The crowd was of a mixed and mingled opinion as to what was happening. Some thought the disciples were day drinking; others thought it was a divine occurrence. Peter addressed the crowd and dropped some knowledge on them: "Men of Judea and all who dwell in Jerusalem, let this be known to you, and give ear to my words. For these people are not drunk, as you suppose.... Hear these words: Jesus of Nazareth, a man attested to you by God with mighty works and wonders and signs that God did through Him in your midst, as you yourselves know—this Jesus, delivered up according to the definite plan and foreknowledge of God, you crucified and killed by the hands of lawless men.... This Jesus God raised up, and of that we all are witnesses" (Acts 2:14–15, 22–23, 32). The nascent Church, as early as Pentecost, was born confessing truth with penetrating clarity.

Clarifying confusion became a full-time job for the Early Church:

- Peter confessed the Gospel to another crowd, this time confused by the healing of a lame man in Solomon's portico: "Men of Israel, why do you wonder at this, or why do you stare at us? . . . The faith that is through Jesus has given the man this perfect health in the presence of you all" (Acts 3:12, 16).

- Stephen spoke the Gospel clearly to a group who had been stirred up on account of mingled truth and falsehood (Acts 6:12–13; 7:2–53).

- Simon the magician was confused about the Holy Spirit—"Now when Simon saw that the Spirit was given through the laying on of the apostles' hands, he offered them money" (Acts 8:18)—until Peter spoke truth to him (Acts 8:20–24).

- An Ethiopian government official was confused about Scripture until Philip clarified the words of Isaiah and the salvation of Jesus (Acts 8:35).

- Paul went from being a confused adversary of the Church to one of its clearest confessors (Acts 9).

The Book of Acts tells how the Holy Spirit worked through the Early Church to clearly confess Jesus in a world of confusion during the first century. This work persisted into the second century and third century. It appears from numerous historical artifacts that there was a great deal of misinformation surrounding the Christian faith. A number of pagan Greco-Roman authors discuss Christians in their various writings. Some simply mention Christians in passing as part of broader conversations about philosophy, science, history, or biographical narratives. These authors include Tacitus, Suetonius, Phlegon, Lucian, Galen, Epictetus, and Marcus Aurelius.[1] Some ancient authors extensively address questions surrounding the Christian faith.

One example comes from letters exchanged by two Roman authorities: Governor Pliny and Emperor Trajan. Their letters reveal the horrific persecution of Christians in the second century. Emperor Trajan had sent Pliny (Gaius Plinius Caecilius Secundus, or Pliny the Younger) to serve as governor to the province of Bithynia on the coast of the Black Sea around AD 110–12. From their correspondence, it appears that misinformation and misunderstandings about Christianity fueled the violence inflicted on the Early Church.

Pliny, seeking advice regarding what to do about the Christians in his jurisdiction, wrote a letter to Trajan saying,

> **In the meantime, this is the plan which I have adopted in the case of those Christians who have been brought before me. I ask them whether they are Christians, if they say "Yes," then I repeat the question the second time, and also a third—warning them of the penalties involved; and if they persist, I order them away to prison.[2]**

There is no indication from either Pliny or Trajan as to the motives or reasoning for imprisoning Christians. Their letters are silent on that matter. However, it is clear that there was widespread confusion about the Christian faith. Pliny writes, "Therefore I placed two women, called 'deaconesses,' under torture, but I found only a debased superstition carried to great lengths."[3] Pliny was convinced—according to whatever he did know or did not know about Christianity—that it was nothing more than superstition.

---

1   See Jakob Engberg, Anders-Christian Jacobsen, and Jörg Ulrich, eds., *In Defence of Christianity: Early Christian Apologists*, trans. Gavin Weakley, Early Christianity in the Context of Antiquity, vol. 15 (Frankfurt am Main: Peter Lang, 2014), 202.

2   William Stearns Davis, ed., *Readings in Ancient History: Illustrative Extracts from the Sources, vol. 2: Rome and the West* (Boston: Allyn and Bacon, 1912–13), 220.

3   Davis, *Readings*, 221.

It appears, though, that even some of those who claimed to be Christian were equally confused about the Christian faith. Pliny developed a test to determine who should or should not be executed. He would order the accused to curse the name of Christ and call upon the gods and sacrifice incense and wine to the image of Emperor Trajan:

> **Those who denied that they were or had been Christians and called upon the gods with the usual formula, reciting the words after me, and those who offered incense and wine before your image—which I had ordered to be brought forward for this purpose, along with the [regular] statues of the gods—all such I considered acquitted. . . . Still others there were, whose names were supplied by an informer. These first said they were Christians, then denied it, insisting they had been, "but were no longer." . . . These all worshiped your image and the god's statues and cursed the name of Christ.[4]**

It would seem from this account that many of the accused individuals, apparently confused about what they believed or why they believed it, acquiesced to the demands of Pliny and denied the Christian faith.

Misinformation and rumors about followers of Jesus had spread through the Roman Empire. Christian apologists set about the task of defending the Christian faith. The word *apologetics* comes from the ancient Greek legal system; the prosecution would offer up an accusation (κατηγορία, *katēgoria*), and the defendant would offer up a defense against these claims (ἀπολογία, *apologia*). In the second and third centuries, engaging in apologetics was not a recreational pastime for Christians; rather, apologetics was a life-and-death endeavor for them. Articulating the truth about Jesus and clarifying confusion about what it means to follow Him kept Diocletian's sword away from your throat and the lions from your limbs.

These early apologists had to winsomely, persuasively, and effectively speak the truth about following Jesus. Many of the apologists of the Early Church were converts to the Christian faith. They had a thorough knowledge of Roman culture, religion, and life because they had been steeped in it for years. They were not speaking about something they did not know;

---

4   Davis, *Readings*, 220–21.

rather, they were defending the Christian faith against the pagan practices in which they themselves had previously engaged.

One of the most well-known apologists of the Early Church was Justin Martyr. His "First Apology" (AD 155–57) sought to clarify the confusion surrounding what it means to follow Jesus. Addressing the Roman emperor Antoninus, Justin writes,

> **For in these pages we do not come before you with flattery, or as if making a speech to win your favor, but asking you to give judgment according to strict and exact inquiry—not, moved by prejudice or respect for superstitious men, or by irrational impulse and long-established evil rumor.[5]**

There were so many prejudices, superstitions, and rumors about Christianity that before Justin could start clarifying the confusion and articulating a confession that is clearly Christian, he wanted to make sure he was going to receive a fair hearing.

Other apologists also went about the work of clarifying the misinformation and rumors. Athenagoras, a convert to Christianity, defended the Christian faith from rumors about incest and cannibalism. In his "A Plea regarding Christians," like Justin Martyr, Athenagoras began his argument with a plea for an impartial hearing. Athenagoras writes,

> **I must at the outset of my defense beg you, illustrious Emperors, to hear me impartially. Do not prejudge the case through being influenced by popular and unfounded rumor, but apply your love of learning and of truth to our cause. Thus you will not be led astray through ignorance, and we, disproving the uncritical rumors of the crowd, shall cease to be persecuted.[6]**

He goes on to deconstruct the rumors about incestuous relationships and cannibal practices happening among the followers of Jesus. Athenagoras demonstrates how Christian beliefs on marriage and life are incongruent with incest and cannibalism.

---

5   Justin Martyr, "The First Apology," trans. Edward Rochie Hardy, *Early Christian Fathers*, vol. 1, The Library of Christian Classics (Philadelphia: Westminster Press, 1953), 242–43, §2.

6   Athenagoras, "A Plea regarding Christians," trans. Cyril C. Richardson, *Early Christian Fathers*, vol. 1, The Library of Christian Classics (Philadelphia: Westminster Press, 1953), 302–3, §2.

Fake news was a real problem for the Early Church. The misinformation about Christians did more than make the neighbors suspicious of the Christians living next door. These rumors were not just idle talk in the city commons. Rather, these controversies led people to reject the Good News of Jesus and persecute anyone who did not do the same. Therefore, apologists like Irenaeus were not speaking hyperbolically when they wrote accounts such as this one:

> **Certain men, rejecting the truth, are introducing among us false stories and vain genealogies, which serve rather to controversies, as the apostle said, than to God's work of building up in the faith. By their craftily constructed rhetoric they lead astray the minds of the inexperienced, and take them captive, corrupting the oracles of the Lord, and being evil expounders of what was well spoken.**[7]

The Early Church dealt with irrational impulses, popular and unfounded rumors, and baseless controversies. The ancient followers of Jesus were engaged in the endless endeavor to separate truth from falsehood, fact from fiction, fake news from the Good News of Christ Jesus.

✕ THE MIDDLE AGES AND THE REFORMATION
– STILL CONFUSED –

One might think that all this confusion came from the Early Church being on the margins of the culture. During the first and second century, the Roman Empire was overtly committed to disrupting the spread of Christianity. During the third century, emperors carried out even more systematic persecution of Christians, such as putting followers of Jesus into colosseums filled with lions; thereby they pushed the Church from the margins into the basement of the culture. Writers, historians, and orators misinformed others about Christian beliefs and practices. It would be logical to assume that all this confusion came from a government and culture dead set against following the living Jesus.

This was not the case. People continued to be confused about Christianity even when the Church was no longer on the fringes of society.

---

7   Irenaeus, "Selections from the Work against Heresies," trans. Edward Rochie Hardy, *Early Christian Fathers*, vol. 1, The Library of Christian Classics (Philadelphia: Westminster Press, 1953), 358, §1.

In the early fourth century, Constantine became the first Christian emperor of the Roman Empire. Having a Christian emperor meant that followers of Jesus could finally emerge from the basement of the culture and the fringes of society. Constantine stopped the widespread persecution of Christians with the Edict of Milan in AD 313. This edict returned previously confiscated Christian property. The Council of Nicaea was convened in AD 325 and allowed Christian leaders from around the empire to openly meet and discuss essential Christian beliefs without fear of persecution.

Yet, even when Christianity became the official state religion of the Roman Empire, the confusion surrounding what it means to be a Christian persisted into the Middle Ages. The theological and political disputes within the Church during this time are evidence that the Christian faith was anything but clear.

FIFTH TO FIFTEENTH CENTURIES

Numerous theological misunderstandings spread through Christianity with viral tenacity. For example, Nestorius (AD 386–ca. 451), a priest and monk living in Syria, confused the incarnation of Christ. This heresy, later called Nestorianism, taught that Jesus existed as two distinct persons (the human Jesus and the divine Son of God) rather than one person (God in human flesh) with two natures. Attempting to correct the confusion of Nestorius, a church leader named Eutyches (AD ca. 380–ca. 456) created his own confusion by overcorrecting the errors of Nestorius. Eutyches argued that Jesus was a fusion of humanity and divinity in which the two natures were turned into a single blended nature that was part human and part divine. These theological misunderstandings, along with many others, led to a series of church councils and creeds to help clarify the confusion.

Disagreements soon developed regarding who had authority to decide theological issues and how doctrinal disputes were to be resolved. This confusion led to the East-West Schism in 1054. There were persistent misunderstandings between church leaders and political leaders. In 1077, Pope Gregory VII and King Henry IV had an epic argument over the issue of power and authority. Their dispute, known as the Investiture Controversy, resulted in Gregory excommunicating Henry. And it ended with Henry walking around barefoot in the middle of the winter to prove his repentance to Gregory. (Basically, this was like a medieval soap opera.) A fog of confusion, misinformation, and rumors still covered the Christian faith.

The Crusades further confused Christianity. Beginning in the late eleventh century and continuing through the thirteenth century, a series of religious wars were fought in an attempt to reclaim the Holy Land. For many, the focus of Christianity shifted toward geopolitical power and procuring wealth. Misinformation and rumors traveled back and forth between Europe and the Holy Land. Peter the Hermit led the People's Crusade (1096) in which he convinced thousands of people that he had a letter from God commissioning a crusade to reclaim the Holy Land for Christendom. Many women and children joined the fight under the assumption that their innocence and purity would give them success in the battle.

This crusade led to numerous other crusades that slowly spiraled into mass confusion. Although many of the details are unclear in historical records, a Children's Crusade appears to have incited bands of young children to seek to reach the Holy Land. The Fourth Crusade (1202–4) culminated in crusaders from the West attacking Constantinople, the Christian capital of the East. Christians fighting other Christians is a painfully obvious example of this mass confusion.

Another source of widespread confusion was a wildly popular medieval text called the Golden Legend (*Legenda Sanctorum*), which stirred a heap of falsehood into Scripture. It appears to have been first compiled sometime around 1260. The book was full of lore and legend about various biblical figures and saints. At various times in the Middle Ages, the Golden Legend was more widely known and consumed than the Bible. This text blurred the line between the historically accurate accounts of Scripture and the fanciful yarns of popular culture.

Injecting these unsubstantiated legends into the historical accounts of Scripture led to widespread confusion. Although the stories contained in this book were referred to as legends (Latin: *legenda*), people did not simply dismiss the stories as tall tales or fables. Unlike modern connotations of *legend*, the medieval usage of this word simply implied that a text was meant to be read aloud. In fact, the book was written to be used by busy priests and preachers looking for vivid sermon illustrations. In some cases, the fabricated stories of the Golden Legend were more widely heard from pulpits than the truth of Scripture.

Sixteenth and Seventeenth Centuries

The confusion of the Middle Ages (roughly the fifth to the fifteenth centuries) gave way to the confusion of the early modern period (sixteenth and seventeenth centuries). One might think that a period in history known as the Renaissance would be marked by enlightened thinking, clear comprehension, and the pursuit of truth. It undoubtedly was a period in human history marked by technological advancements, tremendous art and music, and advancements in education. This was the age of Raphael, Michelangelo, da Vinci, and Machiavelli. But even then, the mingling of truth and falsehood persisted.

The veneer of marble, poetry, and oil paint that ornamented the Renaissance could not hide the festering confusion within Christendom. In the sixteenth century, the average person living in Europe did not know Latin; Latin was the language of the nobility and educated people. Most people knew a vernacular language (e.g., Italian, German, French). However, the Bible and church worship services were in Latin and not the vernacular. This meant that the average person could not read God's Word, nor understand it in preaching and teaching. Most people were left to simply stare at the stained glass windows in order to learn the narrative of Scripture. This caused generations of people to be unaware of the most basic aspects of the Christian faith. Professed followers of Jesus were ignorant when it came to the Lord's Prayer, Apostles' Creed, Ten Commandments, and so forth.

Not surprisingly, not knowing the basics of Scripture led many people to import their own misinformation into Christianity. The truth about Jesus' body being present in Holy Communion was so profoundly misunderstood that some people would actually hold onto the consecrated bread and use it in love potions and health elixirs.[8] Baptism was so profoundly confused that some theologians advocated the forcible Baptism of Jewish children. Salvation had been distorted into a human project predicated on good works and indulgences. The focus of the Christian life was on doing the right things, saying the right words, or buying the right pieces of paper. There was more misinformation than information, more confusion than clarity, more falsehood than truth.

---

8   Gary K. Waite, *Heresy, Magic, and Witchcraft in Early Modern Europe* (London: Palgrave Macmillan, 2003), 4.

This led to a number of reformations within the church. John Wycliffe (1330–84) and Jan Hus (1369–1415) were harbingers for the reforms that took place in the sixteenth and seventeenth centuries. Martin Luther (1483–1546) went about the work of clarifying the truth about the Christian faith when he wrote the Ninety-Five Theses critiquing the church practice of selling indulgences, setting off a series of reform movements throughout Europe. He published instructional handbooks (known as the Small Catechism and the Large Catechism) as a way to assist parents and children, pastors and laity in knowing the most basic teachings of Christianity. Luther engaged in theological discussions (Heidelberg Disputation, Leipzig Debate, Marburg Colloquy) to clarify misinformation within the teachings of the church. He directed the work of crafting confessions of faith such as the Augsburg Confession, the Apology of the Augsburg Confession (remember *apology* means "defense"), and the Smalcald Articles as a way to clearly articulate the Christian faith.

Other reformers followed Luther and also worked to counter the confusion surrounding Christianity. Philip Melanchthon (1497–1560), Ulrich Zwingli (1484–1531), John Calvin (1509–64), and John Knox (1513–72) all engaged in efforts to reform the church. However, while some of these efforts to reduce confusion and restore truth to the church were effective, some of these efforts only injected further misinformation and confusion into Christendom. Even when trying to clarify the confusion, human beings could not agree on the truth. Therefore, the Age of Reformation was a tumultuous time in history. And it led to even more tumultuous times.

THE MODERN AGE AND BEYOND
− HYPERCONFUSION −

Confusion has gained speed and momentum with time. Ever since it furtively entered into creation with Satan's question to Eve (Genesis 3:1), the mingling of truth and falsehood has worsened. As humanity proceeded into the Modern Age, it ambled only further down the path of confusion.

Eighteenth and Nineteenth Centuries

The Age of Enlightenment seemed to have even more potential for clarity than the Renaissance. In some ways, it was a very promising time in human history. Advancements in education, technology, and science began to change society in massive ways. Monarchic rule was rejected throughout Europe, and democracy became the ideal societal configuration. But in many other ways, the Enlightenment was also a time of profound confusion. The past was despised, and the present was celebrated. Christian beliefs like the incarnation, divinity, and resurrection of Jesus started to be widely derided as outlandish, outmoded, and outright silly.

Chaotic pursuits for knowledge and progress ensued throughout the eighteenth and nineteenth centuries. Enlightenment philosophers issued a clarion call for *sapere aude* ("dare to know"). Truth became defined as what a person could prove or could experience for themselves. Human reason became the final arbitrator of reality and truth. Daring to know, however, quickly gave birth to daring to terrorize. This become one of the most brutal periods in European history. The epicenter of this chaos was France. Kings and aristocrats were beheaded. Churches were gutted and dismantled. The Cult of Reason (French: *Culte de la Raison)* became the state-sponsored religion to replace Christianity. Revolution ruled the day; terror ruled the night. The Reign of Terror and the French Revolution were just a few of the bloody events that occurred during this period of confusion.

The smoldering remains of the Age of Enlightenment gave rise to the Industrial Revolution. Europe and North America built factories, invented technologies, and forced children to work in horrific conditions. Steam engines hurried freight over rails and across oceans. Industrialization quickly changed the entire world; continents began trading raw material at a frenetic pace, and distant nations soon became more dependent on one another for commerce. Religious revivals came and went at various times alongside all of this; industrial progress, however, needed no revival because it never waned. The hum of machines in factories, the smoke pouring out of locomotives, and the noxious smell of burning coal filled the air. The fast-forward button had been pressed on the entire Western world. There was no time to think; there was just enough time to create, consume, and continue pressing forward.

Twentieth Century

Worldwide confusion began to go nova around this time in history. World War I (1914–18) raged across entire continents and led to millions of dead soldiers and civilians. Trench warfare created previously unknown horrific conditions whereby soldiers were threatened from head to toe; bullets flew over their heads, and gangrene consumed their feet. As the newly invented mustard gas settled and millions of bodies were buried after the war, the world traipsed further down a path of confusion from 1918 to 1938.

During this time, the authority of Scripture was bombarded by a movement known as higher criticism. While its roots began in universities and seminaries in the eighteenth and nineteenth centuries, higher criticism reached pulpits and living rooms by the early twentieth century. The higher criticism movement argued that the Bible is fundamentally the same as any other text and that it ought to be studied as such. Higher critics taught the Scriptures as human works of literature, not divine. They demythologized and explained away the truth claims and miracles of the Bible, including Jesus' resurrection, in sociological and psychological terms. Darwinian evolution, Freudian psychology, and Nietzschean nihilism were all superimposed over Scripture. As the Roaring Twenties fox-trotted toward the Great Depression, Christianity also imbibed a strange elixir of liberal theology, morality, and sentimentality, with a psychology chaser.

It goes without saying that World War II did not help ameliorate any of the global confusion. Sixty million dead in the course of six years—or 3 percent of the world's population at the time—created horrific confusion. The fallout from this war stretched into all aspects of life: culture, economy, politics, values, philosophy, and Christianity. The optimism of modernism also died with the millions of worldwide human causalities. Postmodernism emerged as a reaction to modernism. Grand narratives, such as that of the Aryan race proposed by the Nazis, were viewed with skepticism and incredulity. Claims of objectivity were replaced with relativism and subjectivity. The notion that truth is completely a cultural construction—"what is true for you is not true for me"—gained traction for the first time in history.

The twentieth and twenty-first centuries proceeded to shift and swirl with increasing chaos: Confusion increased with the passage of time. Wars came and wars went. Viruses gallivanted around the globe. Technology and globalism contorted our sense of time and scale. The most recent and powerful example of this is the invention of the internet. In this history of confusion, each generation has become more and more accustomed to living in a world of confusion.

DISCUSSION QUESTIONS

1. Do you agree or disagree that modern life is riddled with confusion? Why is society reluctant to admit that confusion is so rampant in the modern age?

2. This chapter defines confusion as the mixing together of truth and falsehood, information and misinformation, knowledge and ignorance. What do you like or dislike about that definition? How else could you describe confusion?

3. Why is it important to recognize that the world has always been confused about what Christians believe? Is this realization comforting, frustrating, or something else?

4. Do you agree or disagree that the world is becoming more and more confused? How is it possible to have more and more knowledge yet also be more and more confused?

2

THE WORLD WIDE WEB
OF CONFUSION

The Christian faith has constantly confronted confusion: Ancient Christians had to deal with rulers muddling the Gospel of Jesus Christ with rumors. Reformation Christians had to untangle human philosophy and tradition that had been mingled with the Word of God. Modern Christians had to grapple with higher criticism and its claim that the miracles of Jesus were fake news.

Christians today face a new challenge. The advent of the internet has exponentially fostered confusion greater than ever before. The internet allows for unprecedented perfusion of misinformation. This technology has enabled falsehood, rumors, and fake news to spread at a frenetic pace.

In the ancient world of togas and landline telephones, misinformation spread on a small scale. Someone had to actually engage another person in conversation and speak some sort of inaccuracy or falsehood, thereby furthering the spread of misinformation. Sometimes a large group of people would get together to hear a public oration full of rumors and falsehood. Before the movable type printing press, someone had to actually write letters on a piece of paper by hand to promulgate fake news. Printing presses allowed for larger print runs and the faster spread of misinformation; however, even this was relatively limited compared to what we now experience.

The internet makes these previous modes of communication look quaint. Flowing through the invisible ether, Wi-Fi enables the nearly instantaneous spread of anything—whether information or misinformation, fact or fiction, truth or falsehood. This mysterious fog of data fills our homes, offices, universities, and public spaces. Racing through fiber-optic cables, packets of data disassemble and reassemble faster than the synapses in our brain can fire.

The Christian faith is not impervious to the power of the internet. This technology has radically altered how the world encounters the Gospel of Jesus Christ. Just as ancient Roman roads such as the Appian Way altered how early followers of Jesus traversed the Roman Empire with the Gospel, the internet alters how modern followers of Jesus traverse the world today with the Gospel. This technology has many great affordances for the proc-lamation of the Gospel. The internet has enabled the Good News of Jesus to move around the globe with unprecedented speed and agility. Yet, this technology has also allowed confusion and misinformation about what it means to be a Christian to spread around the globe with unprecedented speed.

In this present moment in human history, the followers of Jesus must find a way to clearly articulate the truth while living in a worldwide web of (mis)information and digital connectivity.

ORIGINS OF THE INTERNET

There are several myths about the origins of the internet. Some people hold to the belief that Al Gore connected the first two Ethernet cables while riding atop a unicorn. Others think the internet came into being when the Cloud began to shower the world with AOL discs. And still others—mostly the members of Generation Z—are convinced that the internet has always existed.

In actuality, the internet is a very new phenomenon. In its brief existence, the internet has profoundly shaped our world. As such, it is important to know something of how the internet got started in the first place. Its origins are in something known as Advanced Research Projects Agency Network (ARPANET). Following the Cold War, the United States Department of Defense began funding efforts to develop a durable communication system. The goal was to create a networked communication system that could withstand enemy disruption efforts. The earliest iteration of the internet was extremely simple and consisted of only a few computers that were connected to one another. The first message conveyed by means of the ARPANET went from a computer at UCLA to a computer at Stanford. On October 29, 1969, computer scientists attempted to send a simple message via the network. The message was supposed to be the word *login*; however, the system crashed on the initial attempt and only transmitted the letters *l* and *o*. Thus with the word *lo*, the internet began.

This early network of computers spawned numerous other similar networks. During the 1970s and 1980s, the earliest form of the internet was used almost exclusively by computer scientists and researchers. Around the 1990s, the internet slowly integrated into broader society. In 1994, Netscape Navigator became one of the first web browsers that enabled easy access to the internet. An increasing number of people had personal computers in their home by this time. The expansion of the internet technology meant an increasing number of people could gain access to the internet for personal use. During that phase, the internet was known as Web 1.0 and largely consisted of static websites with limited opportunities for exchanging messages via discussion boards and email.

Web 2.0 began in the early 2000s and transformed how users engaged the internet. This phase was distinguished by a focus on user-generated content and user interactions. Blogging, wikis, chat rooms, and file-sharing became possible. Many of the popular social media platforms that consume our attention today were born during this time. Facebook had its contentious birth in 2004. YouTube began its video-sharing website in 2005. Twitter hatched and began tweeting in 2006. Instagram started snapping selfies in 2010.

Mobile devices, while distinct from the internet, deserve to be mentioned in any discussion of how the internet has progressed over the years. Roughly around the same time that Web 2.0 began, mobile devices also gained widespread usage. Consumers adopted mobile devices such as smartphones and tablets with incredible speed. Beginning in 2016, the majority of people accessed the internet via mobile devices rather than desktop computers or laptops. This has led to a paradigm shift: creating and using apps on mobile devices as a major component in the nature of the internet.

In a relatively short amount of time—roughly fifty years—the internet has changed everything. It has spawned strange new words such as LOL, meme, GIF, and Googling. It has revolutionized how we interact with one another individually and collectively. The gossamer threads of the internet have stitched the entire world together, and it will never be the same again.

TECHNOLOGY + CULTURE

Digital technology is ubiquitous in modern culture. Very few people go a full day without a digital screen in their face. Numerous estimates have suggested that there will be 50 billion connected devices by the year 2020.[9] If this estimate is correct, then there will be six connected devices for every one human being in the world. Let that sink in for a moment: 50 billion connected devices for the roughly 8 billion human beings.

Smartphones, laptops, tablets, and televisions light our way today. Just as Alice entered Wonderland through a rabbit hole, we enter the world of the internet and digital connectivity through these glowing portals. Rivaling the stars in the sky, these nimbuses of light illuminate our faces and ignite our minds. These modern divining rods accompany us everywhere: Smartphones accompany people to the bedroom and bathroom. Digital tablets supervise young children while parents pay more attention to social media. Laptops outnumber caramel macchiatos at the coffee shop. Televisions tuck us into bed.

The ubiquity of digital technology and internet connectivity calls for an appraisal of its value and impact on society. Is the internet making us smarter? Is the internet making us dumber? Are we better as a result of this emerging technology? Are we worse off because of the internet? If it is making us smarter, does that mean it is good? If it is making us dumber, does that mean it is bad?

It is clear that the internet has been a ferocious force for good. In many regards, the internet is making us smarter as individuals and as a society. The internet has made daily life infinitely easier so that digital banking, online learning, real-time maps and directions, and weather are all at our fingertips. Digital connectivity has provided an unprecedented ability to share and access information.

For example, there used to be these things called libraries. They had something called "business hours," meaning they were closed at certain times of the day. If you wanted to learn about something, you had to go to a library during their business hours and look through an even more ancient artifact called a card catalog. Once you searched the card catalog,

---

9   Ericsson, "CEO to Shareholders: 50 Billion Connections 2020," April 13, 2010, https://www.ericsson.com/en/press-releases/2010/4/ceo-to-shareholders-50-billion-connections-2020.

scanned the library shelves, and eventually found a source that might relate to your area of interest or your question, you had to use an index or a table of contents to try to zero in on the parts of the book that could answer your inquiry. This whole process was time-consuming, inefficient, and laborious. Unlike those things called libraries, the internet never closes or turns off the lights.

Along with unfettered access to information, the internet has allowed for limitless connectivity with others. The cords, cables, and Wi-Fi of the internet link us together with family and friends from around the globe. It has redefined our conceptions of time, space, presence, and friendship. The internet has given us sneezing pandas, dancing babies, and rickrolling. There is no doubt that the internet has been good to us.

Nevertheless, it is clear that the internet has caused many negatives for society. Human trafficking, pornography, cyberbullying, the dark web, and terrorist propaganda have all found a home on the internet. These are clear manifestations of digital connectivity being used for hate, exploitation, and other nefarious activities. There are numerous other negative effects of this technology that are harder for us to discern. Genuine social interaction, quality family time, and undistracted thinking are all threatened by the ever-present siren song of the internet.

Discussions surrounding the value and impact of the internet are part of a larger discourse known as technological determinism. This theory seeks to explain how various technologies exert power on society. There are various lines of thought about the extent to which technology determines our actions and interactions. Some argue that technology is completely neutral—neither good nor bad—and it is solely the user who makes it work for either good or bad. Some argue that technology inclines us toward a certain action and, therefore, is not entirely neutral. For instance, they would say the technology of a paved road inclines a traveler to take a certain route and in so doing that technology exerts power on society. This presumes technology exerts a force on the world by making certain tasks easier or harder. A third approach argues technology is not at all innocuous or passive; rather, it always benefits some people and not others, always exerts some sort of force, creates an order, or determines human behavior. In this version of technological determinism, technology heavily determines the structure and value of society. For instance, the height of an overpass bridge determines whether public transit can use that road, thus determining who can or cannot live in certain parts of a city.

In order to critically engage technology, we must look not only at an object itself, but also at the context in which it is situated. You cannot fully make sense of an automobile without also considering roads, traffic, and human drivers. You cannot fully make sense of the internet without also considering the information, culture, and human users. It is vital to explore both the object (technology) and the context (culture). Only then can we see how each actively shapes the other. Humans formed the internet, yet the internet now forms humanity.

Brains are shaping and shifting to accommodate this flood of new technology. Society is increasingly distracted, impatient, and unreflective. Waiting thirty seconds for a video to buffer is twenty-nine seconds too long. Reading an entire news article online is rare; reflecting on that same news article for any length of time is insane. This digital flow of information has created tempestuous minds that border on addiction: texting while driving, tweeting from the toilet seat, and gaming without eating or sleeping for days on end. Emerging technology has changed our world in a number of critical ways:

Hive Mind: Groupthink, collective intelligence, and mob mentality are all manifestations of hive mind. This uncritical conformity has been normalized by the internet. Social media is a beehive of activity with users buzzing from one post to the next while commenting, liking, and sharing. There is no time to think for oneself or reflect on the ramifications of sharing a post; there are simply too many other posts to pollinate across platforms.

One of the clearest manifestations of hive mind is online shaming. The digital hive finds its target—someone holding to an unpopular view, doing something perceived by others as wrong, or making a simple mistake—and begins to swarm with public condemnation. This may be as innocuous as someone taking up too many seats on public transit or leaving a pet in the car while picking up clothing from the dry cleaners. Photos, videos, and hashtags buzz around the internet as fast as a swarm of bees coalesces around its prey. No time or incentive to think for yourself or consider the individual person being shamed—there is only enough time to swarm, destroy, and move on to the next target.

Fake News: The internet makes creating and publishing content incredibly easy. The cost of entry to become a content creator is little more than a computer and an internet connection. It is also very easy to conceal identity, falsify credentials, or concoct outright falsehoods online. One of the first instances of misinformation on the internet was the infamous Pacific Northwest Tree Octopus. Created in 1998, this internet hoax was a website that blurred the lines between information and misinformation. The fake website contained information about the Pacific Northwest Tree Octopus that appeared to be real. The website described a creature with a scientific-sounding Latin name (*Octopus paxarbolis*), a specific habitat in the Olympic National Forest, and a detailed spawning pattern of the octopus laying eggs in nearby rivers. The website even described the creature's primary predatory threat. (Although it should have been a red flag to readers that its primary predator was Sasquatch.) This conjured cephalopod fooled countless students and internet users; many people came to believe that there was such a thing as the Pacific Northwest Tree Octopus.

This early instance of internet fake news was sadly not the last. Manipulated photos, edited videos, and outright phony reports gallivant around the internet under the guise of legitimate information. Internet literacy has improved since the Pacific Northwest Tree Octopus; people are more discerning concerning the veracity of the information they consume on the internet. Nevertheless, this increased awareness of fake news on the internet has not completely solved the problem. People continue to read, share, and cite misinformation and fake news on the internet.

Participatory Culture: Perhaps the most profound way that the internet has changed our world has to do with participatory culture. The advent of Web 2.0 enabled users to get involved on the internet by contributing and producing content. Participatory culture encourages us to create and share our own viewpoints and perspectives online, rather than simply consume information and ideas. This means that everyone online has a voice. If you can tweet, post, comment, or share, then you can participate on the internet. This has been a powerful force for democracy and justice.

However, the rise of participatory culture has led to a pervasive cultural problem. The call to comment, opine, and rant online has utterly eroded our ability to think deeply and reflect for a sustained period of time. Seldom do people read an entire article online before commenting or sharing. Rarely do people allow more than two mental synapses to fire before reacting to a social media post. Scarcely does anyone ponder something read online for longer than a day. Society is eager to participate online, yet reluctant to reflect. Reaction is prioritized over reflection.

Because the internet has profoundly changed the way we access information and communicate with one another, the world is increasingly confused about what Christians believe and why they believe it.

CONFUSION + CHRISTIANITY IN A DIGITAL AGE

Walk into any college campus, commuter train, or local coffee shop and you will find someone holding to serious misunderstandings about what it means to follow Jesus. These individuals are sitting next to you at work or standing on the sidelines with you during your child's soccer game. These individuals may even be in your own family. Depending on where you are reading this book, the people around you at this very moment may be included in this group. It does not matter where you look; you will find someone who is unclear about the Christian faith.

Our culture is convinced that it knows what it means to be Christian. Our culture thinks that it has a perfectly clear and accurate understanding of the Christian faith. Many people think that it goes something like this:

> Being a Christian is about being a good person, rejecting the physical world, following old-fashioned traditions, judging others, and checking your brain at the front door of the church. The followers of Jesus are heaven-bent on finding happiness, being overly political, and winning arguments. If you want to be part of this community, then you must subscribe to these tenets.

This is a problem. This is a misunderstanding of the Christian faith. Countless people have given up on Christianity without really knowing what it is. They know enough to know that they do not want to know any more. Many of your neighbors, classmates, co-workers, and family members do not know clearly what it means to be a follower of Jesus.

Who or what is the source of all these misunderstandings? Assigning blame for this problem is difficult. It could be that people do not care enough to form an accurate assessment of what it means to be Christian; many individuals reject Christianity on the basis of poorly formed assumptions rather than legitimate knowledge. It may be that the swirl of misinformation clouding Christianity is coming from that deep sea of ignorance within social media; there is an infinite number of misinformed people creating an infinite number of tweets and memes misrepresenting Jesus. It may be that this confusion is the result of fake news and false websites, like the Pacific Northwest Tree Octopus website; perhaps people are uncritically consuming falsified websites about Christianity. Or it may even be that atheism is to blame for all the misunderstanding surrounding the Christian faith.

Maybe.

Or could there be another explanation? Is it possible that Christians are partially responsible for the lack of clarity surrounding the Christian faith? Is it possible that our cloudy confessions have created a confused Christianity? Have our failures cast a pall over the faith and conveyed a murky message about what we believe? Have we obscured Christianity through our hypocrisy and inaction? Have we failed to be clearly Christian?

Certainly.

As discussed in the previous chapter, confusion and sin go together like cat memes and the internet; you cannot have one without the other. Followers of Jesus have never claimed to be sinless people. The Church is not composed of blameless believers who always say, think, and do the right things. As the history of Christianity reveals, resisting the confusion of sin is an ongoing struggle for each generation of believers. We are constantly resisting the work of Satan as he whispers, "Did God actually say?" (Genesis 3:1). We also are perpetually untangling human philosophy and tradition as they try to weave their way into the Word of God. We live in a world that mixes and mingles falsehood and opinion with the truth of God. To be certain, Christians do not always get it right.

Confusion comes from sin. As long as the world has been broken by sin, confusion has sought to destroy the clear confession of the Gospel. Sin knows no boundaries, and therefore confusion knows no boundaries. It happens outside the church in secular society, and it happens inside the church among the followers of Jesus. Misinformation about what it means to be a Christian comes from outside and inside. Others do not know what we believe, and we do not always know what we believe. Others twist our confessions of faith, and we also twist our confessions of faith sometimes. Not all the misinformation about Christianity is coming from some Eastern European fake-news factory. Some of it is coming from our own confusion and misinformation.

So, what do we do?

Jesus' counsel to the Church in Laodicea in Revelation tells us exactly what to do:

> **I know your works: you are neither cold nor hot. Would that you were either cold or hot! So, because you are lukewarm, and neither hot nor cold, I will spit you out of My mouth. For you say, I am rich, I have prospered, and I need nothing, not realizing that you are wretched, pitiable, poor, blind, and naked. I counsel you to buy from Me gold refined by fire, so that you may be rich, and white garments so that you may clothe yourself and the shame of your nakedness may not be seen, and salve to anoint your eyes, so that you may see. Those whom I love, I reprove and discipline, so be zealous and repent. Behold, I stand at the door and knock. If anyone hears My voice and opens the door, I will come in to him and eat with him, and he with Me. The one who conquers, I will grant him to sit with Me on My throne, as I also conquered and sat down with My Father on His throne. He who has an ear, let him hear what the Spirit says to the churches. (Revelation 3:15–22)**

Refuse to be lukewarm and indifferent. Trust not in the riches of our modern technology, knowledge, or wealth. Receive the true riches of God's truth, and let Him clothe us in righteousness, wisdom, and life. Repent and turn away from sin and confusion. Feast on the Word of God, dwell in the presence of Christ Jesus, and hear what the Spirit says.

This is the only way forward for living as followers of Jesus in a world of confusion. This is nothing new. Rather, this is what the followers of Jesus have always been called to do: oppose confusion by being clearly Christian.

DISCUSSION QUESTIONS

1. What are some ways that you have noticed the internet changing our world? Do you agree that the world will never be the same again as a result of the internet? How has the internet changed the way we proclaim the Gospel?

2. Have you ever met someone who held a completely inaccurate understanding of the Christian faith? How did this person come to believe this misinformation? How did you help to clarify the confusion?

3. What are some ways in which individual followers of Jesus contribute to the confusion surrounding the Christian faith?

4. How does Revelation 3:15–22 apply to modern Christians? How are these words both warning and encouragement?

CLEARING THE CONFUSION

Part 2

3

GOOD

Weight-loss programs are all the same. It does not matter if a program is about cutting carbs, counting calories, or eating nothing but crackers and water. It makes no difference if the program requires you to sweat to oldies, hip-hop, or a book on tape. Spandex or sweatpants, protein or vegetables, liquid cleanse or nothing but beef jerky for seven days—weight-loss programs are all the same.

Every weight-loss program is about you doing the right activities, eating the correct food, and choosing to be a healthier person. It is always something you do or a change you must make. It may seem as if weight-loss programs are not all the same. Each program has its own celebrity claiming that you should follow this particular plan. Each program has its own special focus or emphasis that supposedly guarantees success. Each program believes that this super food is the key to reaching your goals.

Nevertheless, despite these surface differences, every single weight-loss program is the same. If you do this in the right way, then you will be a new person. If you work hard and try your best, then you will be rewarded with the beach body you always wanted. If you put in the sweat, then you will get the results.

Our culture likens Christian faith to a spiritual weight-loss program. Our culture thinks that rather than seeking to shed a few extra pounds, Christians are seeking to shed moral imperfections. You join a church for many of the same reasons you join a gym: you want to improve yourself and be a better person. You follow Jesus—a program that has proven to be successful—in order to learn how to get rid of unwanted greed, envy, pride, and worry. You work hard at being a Christian, and slowly you become a good person. And if you do what you are supposed to do, then you will be rewarded in the afterlife with a heavenly all-you-can-eat buffet.

CHRISTIANITY IS FOR BAD PEOPLE

Christianity is not about trying to be a good person. The central message of Christianity, the Gospel of Jesus Christ, is not aimed at good people. That sounds strange. What do you mean Christianity is not about being a good person? Of course it is! Being a Christian means doing your best, trying to be moral, judging others for not being moral, and always letting people merge into your lane during a traffic jam. Right? Wrong.

Jesus did not come to make good people better. Jesus did not come to help bad people learn how to become good people. Jesus did not come to give good advice or proclaim a message of moral perfection. He was not even hawking a newfangled spiritual fitness plan. Jesus came to proclaim Good News to bad people.

This is not a modern misunderstanding. The idea that being a follower of Jesus is synonymous with being a good person is a perennial problem. The world has always been prone to misunderstanding Jesus and His teachings. Nevertheless, even a brief study of the Gospels reveals that Jesus welcomed the worst of the worst into His kingdom. Throughout the Gospels, Jesus made it clear that the purpose of His ministry was to proclaim Good News to bad people.

A TAX COLLECTOR

Jesus called Levi to follow Him at the onset of His public ministry (Mark 2:14). Levi was not a good person according to both the Jewish and Roman cultures of his day. Even his own mother would have likely been dissatisfied with his career choice. Levi was a Jewish man working as a tax collector for the Roman Empire. This means that both groups viewed him with deep suspicion.

Tax collectors helped people lose weight by emptying their pockets. Levi collected the taxes the Romans required from the Jewish people. Nobody likes paying taxes. And these taxes were particularly frustrating. The taxes paid by the Jewish people helped pay for the Roman soldiers occupying their land. As if that was not frustrating enough, tax collectors were known for taking far more than was required. By skimming a little here and a little there, Levi was able to make a substantial income by stealing from his own people.

Jesus did the unthinkable by inviting this dishonest, detested, and despicable tax collector to follow Him as one of His twelve disciples: "And as He passed by, He saw Levi the son of Alphaeus sitting at the tax booth, and He said to him, 'Follow Me.' And he rose and followed Him" (Mark 2:14). As if having a tax collector as a disciple was not scandalous enough, Jesus then went to Levi's house for a meal. Jesus' behavior of hanging out with bad people—sinners and tax collectors—raised some questions among the scribes and Pharisees. They wanted to know why Jesus was eating with these kinds of people. Jesus answered their question by making it clear that He came to proclaim Good News to bad people: "Those who are well have no need of a physician, but those who are sick. I came not to call the righteous, but sinners" (Mark 2:17). The Divine Physician, Christ Jesus, came to heal the spiritually broken and morally depraved.

A Weeping Woman

Scripture does not give us her name. It would seem as if few people cared to even know her name. It seems she is known entirely by her sin. It defines her, describes her, and determines her standing within the neighborhood. Jesus was dining in the house of a Jewish leader. It was the custom in that culture to leave the door to the house open when having a party. People from the city were allowed to enter and be part of the celebration. Well, kind of. Uninvited guests did not have a seat at the table, they were not supposed to interact with the guests of honor, and they could only eat the scraps from the table. A sinful woman, most likely a prostitute, entered the dinner party of this Jewish leader and began to wash the feet of Jesus. Out of reverence for Him, she used her tears for water and her hair for a towel.

This was a problem for the guy throwing the party. He said, "If this man were a prophet, He would have known who and what sort of woman this is who is touching Him, for she is a sinner" (Luke 7:39). Translation: Bad people are not supposed to touch Jesus, come near Him, or cry at His feet. Jesus responded to His host's critique by telling a story about two debtors and a moneylender. One of the debtors owed five hundred denarii, and the other owed fifty denarii. In a moment of unimaginable mercy, the moneylender forgave the debts of both. Jesus then asked His host: "Now which of them will love him more?" (Luke 7:42). The host correctly answered: clearly the one with the greater debt had a greater reason to celebrate this act of mercy.

Moving from the abstract story about mercy to the weeping woman with the alabaster flask of ointment, Jesus proclaimed Good News to a bad person. He said, "Your sins are forgiven" (Luke 7:48).

A Crucified Criminal

The Roman Empire did not crucify every criminal. Jaywalking or driving your donkey over the speed limit did not call for crucifixion. Instead, the Roman Empire used this horrific punishment for only the worst criminals. Typically, this meant political insurrectionists, terrorists, or anyone else posing a serious threat to the empire. Scripture reports that there were two men crucified alongside Jesus. The Gospel writers do not tell us what crime those men committed. However, it is safe to say that they were not hanging on a cross for downloading music illegally. Whatever the crime that earned them death by crucifixion, it is clear that these men were not the models of first-century morality.

One of the men hanging on the cross used his final gasping breaths to mock Jesus (Luke 23:39). The other man, however, said something very different to Jesus: "Jesus, remember me when You come into Your kingdom" (Luke 23:42). And even as His own breaths were becoming labored and shallow, Jesus proclaimed Good News to a bad person: "Truly, I say to you, today you will be with Me in paradise" (Luke 23:43).

The point is this: Jesus did not proclaim Good News to good people. He proclaimed the coming of the kingdom of God to the most broken and dejected sinners. He spoke the forgiveness of sins to the worst offenders. He welcomed the most ostracized and rejected members of society. And He does the very same for you.

THERE ARE NO GOOD PEOPLE

Christians believe that there is no such thing as an intrinsically good person. The notion that people are more good than bad belongs in the realm of fairy tales. You are more likely to find a leprechaun riding on top of a unicorn being led by Paul Bunyan than you are to find a truly good person. Wishful thinking may delude us into believing that good prevails within us. Yet, it is abundantly clear that this is not true. That sounds pretty harsh, doesn't it? Let me explain.

Imagine if you had a few computers in front of you and your job was to determine which ones were good and which ones were bad. In order to accomplish this task, you spend some time working with each computer. One is missing the power cord and fails to even start. It is dead. One turns on and goes immediately to the "blue screen of death," indicating a serious problem. Another computer powers up and allows you to view the desktop. Clicking on a program, however, results in an hour of watching a tiny hourglass do nothing. These computers all are clearly bad.

Then you encounter a computer that *appears* to be better than the others. It powers up, loads programs, and seemingly does what a computer is supposed to do. It allows you to write a document, send an email, and access the internet. There is one serious problem though: The computer never actually does what it is supposed to do. It is as if the computer has a mind of its own. It always chooses to go its own way and do what it wants to do. If you try to save a document in one folder, the computer puts it in another folder. If you try to send an email to one person, the computer sends it to someone else in your contact book. If you type in the URL for one website, the computer takes you to another website. It appears to be doing what a computer is supposed to do; however, it is really doing nothing that a computer is supposed to do.

Would you call this computer good? No. It is not functioning as it is supposed to function. It does not do what it was designed to do. It is rebellious and wayward, and its internal coding is warped and twisted. What may look like a good computer is in fact a bad computer.

Christians believe that humanity is a lot like these bad computers: "They have all turned aside; together they have become corrupt; there is none who does good, not even one" (Psalm 14:3). Christians believe that sin has taken what is good—humanity and God's creation—and made it bad. Sin injects a lethal dose of chaos, confusion, decay, and death into this world.

Dead: Like the first computer that was dead without a power cord, we are dead in sin: "And you were dead in the trespasses and sins" (Ephesians 2:1). Sin and death are inextricably linked; because all people are sinful, all people are subject to the power of death. No matter how good a person may seem, the bad news of death is a reality.

Infected: Like the second computer that went straight into malfunction, we are full of infection and disease: "But each person is tempted when he is lured and enticed by his own desire. Then desire when it has conceived gives birth to sin, and sin when it is fully grown brings forth death" (James 1:14–15). The malicious virus of sin plagues us all. Sin attacks God's good creation, rewrites how we operate, and infects all that we do.

Incapable: Like the third computer that stalled out loading applications, we are unable to do what is truly good: "For the mind that is set on the flesh is hostile to God, for it does not submit to God's law; indeed, it cannot" (Romans 8:7). Sin leaves us utterly incapable of doing what is truly good. Sin corrupts even our best intentions and purest desires.

Rebellious: Like the fourth computer that appeared to be good but was actually bad, we may appear to be good but are actually bad: "There is a way that seems right to a man, but its end is the way to death" (Proverbs 14:12). Even when people do things that appear to be good, they are actually misguided deeds masquerading as good.

Although humanity was made good, we have become bad. God's creation was thoroughly good: "And God saw everything that He had made, and behold, it was very good" (Genesis 1:31). Despite being made good, Adam and Eve embraced bad and rebelled against God. The virus of sin entered in and corrupted it all. Sin has rewritten the coding underlying creation so that what was once good has become bad. Not kind of bad. Not a little bad. Not more good than bad. Truly and completely bad and broken, dead and mangled. Christians believe that we are all bad people in need of Good News.

GOOD NEWS ≠ GOOD ADVICE

How does a bad computer become a good computer? If a computer is dead on account of a faulty power cord or battery, it must have the old one taken out and a new one put in its place. If the processor is malfunctioning, then it must be replaced with a fully functioning processor. If the screen is cracked, then an unblemished screen must be put in its place. If the software is glitchy, then new code must be written over the old code. A mere software patch will not fix a serious underlying problem. The broken parts must be replaced. The old must be swapped out with the new. That is the only way.

How do bad people become good people? God takes the bad and replaces it with good. God removes the old and installs the new. God provides all that is needed to become truly and completely good.

The Bible is God proclaiming Good News to bad people. God's promises pervade Scripture; they penetrate the bad news of a broken world and provide hope in Christ Jesus. The Bible is not primarily moral teachings. It is the proclamation of God that He has come to make all things new: "Therefore, if anyone is in Christ, he is a new creation. The old has passed away; behold, the new has come" (2 Corinthians 5:17).

Good news is not to be confused with good advice. Good advice is a suggestion for how you might live better: Spend less than you make. Buy low and sell high. An apple a day keeps the doctor away. You can pick your friends, you can pick your nose, but you cannot pick your friend's nose. These are all examples of good advice. Good advice is a directive for how you ought to live or a change that you need to make. Good news is different. News announces something that has happened. News tells of something that has already occurred and now changes how we relate to the past, the present, and the future. News—especially big news—changes the world forever. Here are just a few examples of big news that changed the world:

December 11, 1241: The Mongol warrior Batu Khan, grandson of Genghis Khan, was on a military campaign approaching Vienna. He was well poised for widespread victory and would have likely destroyed the Holy Roman Empire. However, it was on this day that Ögedei Khan, the second Great Khan of the Mongol empire, died. Rather than destroying Vienna and marching clear to the Atlantic, the news of the death forced Batu Khan to return to

Mongolia so that he could discuss the succession. The news of Ögedei Khan's death forever changed European history.

October 24, 1929: Known as Black Thursday, this was the day on which the Wall Street Crash of 1929 began to spiral downward out of control. The market lost 11 percent of its value on this day. This fueled further losses in the market. As the news of this occurrence spread to investors around the world, panic ensued; a number of people even committed suicide. Past investments became a present catastrophe as the future headed toward the Great Depression.

September 2, 1945: This was the day on which military leaders from Japan and the United States of America signed the documents of surrender that effectively ended World War II. The news of this event changed the past, the present, and the future. As this news spread, it changed how people related to the past sacrifices of countless soldiers, the present turmoil in Europe, and the hope for peace in the future.

Notice how there is no advice to be had in these examples of big news. There are no suggestions for how to improve your life or realize your full potential. There is no recommendation for creating better habits or making more friends. Rather, news conveys what has happened in human history. News reports events and occurrences, not advice or opinions. Hearing the news of these occurrences changes how people relate to the past, present, and future.

The Gospel is the Good News of the life, death, and resurrection of Jesus Christ. This Good News proclaims that God has come into human history and forever changed the past, present, and future of this world. Jesus has vanquished on the cross the past reality of death, decay, sin, and suffering. He has come into creation and brought healing and salvation into the present. And He has secured your future hope through the power of the empty tomb. Your past, present, and future are forever changed as a result of the Good News of Jesus.

Christianity is not morality. It is not a ten-step program to becoming a good person. Christianity is the Good News of Jesus Christ proclaimed to bad people.

GOOD, BAD, OR BOTH?

The news that salvation has come in Christ Jesus changes your past, present, and future. Your past sins have been left for dead in the tomb. Your present failings are swallowed up in the mercy of Jesus. Your future is forever changed as a result of Jesus. This is really good news for you.

Jesus makes all things new: He takes what is bad and makes it good. He takes what is dead and makes it alive. He takes what is wrong and makes it right. Being a Christian means that through faith you have Christ in you: "I have been crucified with Christ. It is no longer I who live, but Christ who lives in me. And the life I now live in the flesh I live by faith in the Son of God, who loved me and gave Himself for me" (Galatians 2:20).

There is a common misconception when it comes to Christian morality. People often assume that a certain moral threshold must be surpassed before one becomes a Christian. The prevailing idea goes like this: if you can live according to the moral standards of Christianity, then you can rightfully call yourself a Christian. The thought is you must fall somewhere on the left of the dotted line on the good/bad continuum before you are good enough to be a Christian.

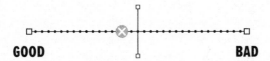

GOOD   **BAD**

This is incorrect. This assumes that one can become moral enough to become a Christian. But morality does not make you a Christian. Jesus does. He proclaims good news to bad people. His perfection is counted as our perfection despite our deep imperfections. His righteousness is counted as our righteousness despite our overwhelming inability to do anything that is truly right. His good work is considered our good work despite our bad accomplishments. The visual below is a more accurate depiction of Christianity.

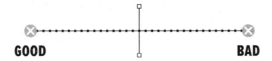

GOOD   **BAD**

Christians believe that they are simultaneously good and bad. Not half good and half bad. Not sometimes good and sometimes bad. Not a little more good than bad. We are both good and bad at the same time.

Christ Jesus makes us good. Having Jesus dwelling in us through faith means that His perfect holiness is ours. Through faith in Christ Jesus, His righteousness is credited to us; we are made perfect, but only because He is perfect (Romans 4:13–24). His good works are the only thing truly good in us; we have nothing to boast about other than Christ Jesus (Ephesians 2:8–9). Christ makes bad people good. Not kind of good. Not barely good. He makes us fully and entirely good.

And yet, we recognize that we are fully and truly bad apart from Christ Jesus. We are by nature dead, infected, incapable, and rebellious until the end of our earthly lives. Nothing good can dwell in us apart from the goodness of God:

> **For I know that nothing good dwells in me, that is, in my flesh. For I have the desire to do what is right, but not the ability to carry it out. For I do not do the good I want, but the evil I do not want is what I keep on doing. Now if I do what I do not want, it is no longer I who do it, but sin that dwells within me. (Romans 7:18–20)**

We are utterly incapable of overcoming sin and carrying out what is good.

Rightfully understood, Christians see themselves as simultaneously being at both ends of the spectrum. We know the bad that dwells in us and refuse to delude ourselves into thinking that we are good people. We do not try to justify ourselves, piling up good deeds and platitudes in a feeble attempt to feel better about ourselves. We can openly and honestly admit that we are bad people full of gluttony, lies, and avarice.

Being a Christian is acknowledging that we are bad yet God has been good to us in Christ Jesus: "Wretched man that I am! Who will deliver me from this body of death? Thanks be to God through Jesus Christ our Lord!" (Romans 7:24–25). We praise God that He has come to proclaim Good News to bad people.

Does this mean that Christians do not care at all about how they live? Is the Christian life nothing more than a divine hall pass granting permission to sin freely? No. Having been restored in Christ Jesus, the Christian life includes the Holy Spirit working in the lives of believers to make them holy. The next chapter will explore how being made good in Jesus does change how Christians live in the world. New life in Christ means living in a completely new way here and now. Christianity is not an only spiritual salvation that is disconnected from daily life.

CONCLUSION

Following Jesus is not a program for spiritual betterment. Being a Christian is not about trying your best. Jesus never said that He came to make good people better, nice people nicer, or holy people holier. Jesus came for bad people. And that means that Jesus came for all people.

Christianity's claim that people are inherently bad is radically countercultural. Our culture is convinced that people are inherently good, and bad people are the exception. Christianity holds to exactly the opposite belief: people are inherently sinful, and God alone is good. He takes what is bad and makes it good. He is our goodness. We have no room to boast of anything because the good that we do is not our own. Jesus came to dead, infected, incapable, rebellious people. And He came to proclaim healing and new life for all.

Clear > Confusion = **MORE JESUS**

More cowbell. This pop-culture catchphrase comes from a television comedy sketch that aired in the early 2000s. The sketch depicts a band recording a song in a studio. All of the band members are playing their instruments at a reasonable volume . . . except for the guy on the cowbell. He is playing his instrument way, way too loud. The producer stops the song in the middle of recording. It appears that he is going to chastise the cowbell player for overpowering all the other instruments. Instead, the producer tells the band that there is something wrong with how they are playing the song. Something is missing in the song. It needs more cowbell. No matter how loud the cowbell player performs, the producer keeps advising the band to use more cowbell.

More Jesus. All kidding aside, that is really good advice for how to be clearly Christian in our age of confusion. We often let other elements of the Christian faith drown our proclamation of Jesus: It is easy to tell other people how much we love our church or Bible study group. It is no problem for us to talk to our neighbors about how we sing in the choir, volunteer at the coat bank, or read the Bible. We regale others at work with stories about how bad the world has become, all the while implying that we are morally better than those people. We post on social media about the upcoming potluck or to ask for prayers for Aunt Millie's goiter or our pet dog's arthritis. And we present all of this—church potlucks, prayer requests, commentary on the deplorable state of the world and other people—as the sum and total of Christianity.

Then we are confused why people are confused about Christianity.

Why do they think being Christian is only about attending church potlucks and choir rehearsals? How come so many people think that the Christian faith is about trying to be a good person? Why do people think that being a Christian means you must be morally superior to others?

Perhaps we—and they—need more Jesus. More Jesus in our casual conversations with neighbors and colleagues. More Jesus in how we describe the Christian faith at work or school. More Jesus in our social media posts and digital interactions. More Jesus in everything.

The apostle Paul, sort of like the producer advising more and more cowbell, was in favor of more Jesus: "And I, when I came to you, brothers, did not come proclaiming to you the testimony of God with lofty speech or wisdom. For I decided to know nothing among you except Jesus Christ and Him crucified" (1 Corinthians 2:1–2). Instead of leading off with lofty speech and profound wisdom, Paul emphasized more Jesus. Instead of highlighting the periphery details, we can focus on the Christ part of Christianity. Rather than proclaiming potlucks and morality, we can proclaim how God has come to seek and save bad people.

How can we make it clear that Christianity is about Good News and not good advice? How can we place more emphasis on Jesus? There are a number of ways that we can do this—both in person and online in this digital age:

Lead with Jesus: What you lead off with is vitally important. Journalists often structure stories in the form of an inverted pyramid. The main and most important point comes first, then other important details, and finally other general information and details come at the end of the story. This inverted pyramid structure allows readers to quickly find the main point of a news article without having to hack through a jungle of details. Similarly, the people of Jesus should lead with the main and most important point—Jesus. Instead of leading with our morality, saintliness, or righteousness, try leading with Jesus. After all, He is the main and most important point of the Christian faith. Journalists are taught not to bury the lead. In other words, do not let the most important point get buried in the details. Lead with Jesus in your face-to-face and digital interactions, and you can be certain that others will hear the main point of being Christian.

Own the Blame, Give God the Glory: Have you ever met someone who accepts all the accolades yet passes all the blame to others? Yeah, that person is kind of annoying. Followers of Jesus must be cautious not to act or speak as if they deserve any of the glory for their salvation. The truth of the matter is that we deserve all the blame on account of our sin. And Jesus deserves all the glory for our salvation. God alone should get all the glory for our accomplishments and successes—whatever they are. In subtle and sometimes not-so-subtle ways, we seek to give ourselves the glory. Rather than humblebragging on ourselves, let's just straight up brag on God: "Let the one who boasts, boast in the Lord" (1 Corinthians 1:31).

Rethink Social Media: We have great control over the image of ourselves that we construct online. Rather than presenting our real self, we prefer to show the world an edited version of ourselves. It is rare that someone posts a picture of their messy living room; it is even rarer that someone posts anything having to do with their messy mistakes, sins, and failures. Why? Because that would be awkward and out of place in social media communities. The majority of people do not even hint at their shortcomings online. Nevertheless, if we all keep crafting a fake version of ourselves online, we are creating an environment where no one seems to need Jesus. This does not mean that we have to bear our heart and soul on social media and make everyone uncomfortable as they scroll by our posts. Instead, find a way to make a small gesture toward being honest as a forgiven sinner online. This is not just digital self-deprecation; this is admitting your deficiencies and need for a Savior, regardless of the format and medium. You will be amazed at how quickly Jesus comes up when we stop acting like we have life all figured out.

More Jesus. This is really good advice in a digital age full of noise and confusion. In a culture that is unclear about the Christian faith, the people of Jesus need to be overwhelmingly clear: Jesus is the indispensable core of Christianity.

DISCUSSION QUESTIONS

1. This chapter describes several instances of Jesus proclaiming Good News to a bad person. What other examples of this are there in Scripture? What do these examples tell us about Jesus?

2. Sin has made us all bad. Yet, the notion of sin is unpopular and largely rejected by contemporary culture. How does our contemporary culture depict humanity? According to the world, are people mostly good, mostly bad, or somewhere in between? How does the world determine who or what is good, bad, or in between?

3. Have you ever experienced someone confusing the Good News of Jesus with merely good advice?

4. What are other ways that you can have more Jesus in everything? Do you find it easier to talk to others about the periphery parts of Christianity rather than simply talking about Jesus?

SPIRITUAL

---

*"For God so despised the world, that He
gave His only Son that whoever believes
in Him should escape the physical world
and play a harp in the clouds."*

Christians are only concerned with spiritual things.
They reject the physical world and rely only on what
is unseen: faith, prayer, angels, heaven, and God. They
believe that God works exclusively in spiritual ways
that are mystically perceived rather than touched, tast-
ed, or seen. Christians look suspiciously on anything
that is physical, tangible, or earthy. They believe that
the body is far less important than the soul. They look
forward to an eternal existence where they float on
clouds, singing like angels, and are finally freed from
their physical bodies. And Christians believe that every
time a bell rings an angel gets its wings.

Christians do not actually believe any of these things. These are distortions of the Christian faith. Our culture wrongfully assumes that these are
core confessions found on every page of the Bible and believed by every

Christian. The truth is that you are more likely to find these beliefs in classical philosophy or on the internet than in Scripture.

Jesus never said that the spiritual is more important than the physical. Jesus never taught that the soul is the only thing that matters and that the body does not matter all that much. Jesus never once denied the significance and importance of God's physical creation.

Plato did.

JESUS ≠ PLATO

Athens was the hub of philosophy in ancient Greece. You could not spit without hitting a bearded philosopher endlessly speculating on the nature of reality. Plato (fourth century BC) is one of the most influential philosophers to have come out of Athens. Plato supposedly studied under Socrates and wrote down many of Socrates's teachings. Aristotle studied the teachings of Plato as part of his academy. Plato's influence is so profound that many people have claimed all philosophy is a footnote to his philosophy. His thinking—known as Platonism—has left an indelible mark on the world.

Platonism teaches that the spiritual world is superior to the physical world. This teaching is explained in *The Republic* through a story known as the "allegory of the cave." Plato invites readers to imagine there were people living in a cave. These people had never ventured outside of the cave because they were chained to the walls. All they can see are shadows cast on the wall of the cave as things pass in front of a fire that is behind them. They eventually give names to these shadows and assume that they are the full experience of reality. If it were possible for these people to be released from the chains confining them to the cave, then they would quickly realize that what they understood as reality was nothing more than shadows.

According to Platonism, the allegory of the cave illustrates how people wrongfully assume that the physical world is reality when in fact it is merely a shadow of reality. Nonphysical forms are the basis for physical objects. For instance, the idea of a perfect circle exists in the nonphysical world, yet all physical circles are just imperfect shadows of the ideal circle. (The word *ideal* is based on the Platonic notion that nonphysical *ideas* are the standard for reality.) Platonism teaches that what is physical is inferior to what is nonphysical—the spiritual is always greater than the physical.

Jesus was not a student of Plato. Jesus never once cited Plato, endorsed his views, or espoused a Platonic worldview. Jesus did not disparage God's physical creation.

Rather than rejecting the physical creation, Jesus got His holy hands dirty with the stuff of the earth. God so loved the physical world that He entered into it by taking on flesh and blood, muscle and sinew, in Christ Jesus. He ate the food of the earth, drank the water flowing in streams, and walked the dusty streets of Galilee. He was baptized in the tawny, warm water of the Jordan River. He took bread and wine, crafted from grain and grapes grown in the ground, and gave them to His disciples saying, "Take, eat; this is My body. . . . Drink of it, all of you, for this is My blood of the covenant, which is poured out for many for the forgiveness of sins" (Matthew 26:26–28).

God fully and completely engaged His physical creation in Christ Jesus. The life, death, and resurrection of Jesus makes it abundantly clear that God is deeply concerned with both the spiritual and physical realms of His creation.

INCARNATION

"And the Word became flesh and dwelt among us" (John 1:14). God taking on human flesh and dwelling within creation reveals the importance of the physical realm. The incarnation of Christ Jesus was not an illusion or chimera. It was the real union of God and humanity. Divinity combined with deoxyribonucleic acid. The Son of God submerged in amniotic fluid within the womb. The blood of human birth as a precursor to the blood that would one day be shed on the cross for the sins of the world. There were the cries of human life as Jesus emerged from the womb and gasped the air of creation, the very air that was made in and through Him in the beginning. The incarnation of Jesus stands as a bulwark against any claim that Christianity is reluctant to embrace the physical world.

Nevertheless, the incarnation of Jesus has been a contentious teaching throughout the history of Christianity. Paul had to clearly articulate the reality of the incarnation: "But when the fullness of time had come, God sent forth His Son, born of woman" (Galatians 4:4). Ignatius of Antioch (AD 35–107), an apologist in the Early Church, defended the truth of the incarnation against false claims: "There is only one physician—of flesh yet spiritual, born yet unbegotten, God incarnate, genuine life in the midst of death, sprung from Mary as well as God, first subject to suffering then beyond it—Jesus Christ our Lord."[10] Followers of Jesus have always recognized the incarnation of Jesus as being a powerful example of God's willingness to engage the physical realm of creation.

Teaching

The teachings of Jesus provide further proof that the physical realm of creation matters to God. The Sermon on the Mount (Matthew 5) makes it clear that what happens in the physical realm is important. There is no indication here that Jesus is only concerned with a person's spiritual disposition. Rather, Jesus takes up very earthly matters: anger, lust, divorce, oaths, retribution, and earthly enemies. Elsewhere, Jesus taught His followers how to pray and included earthly matters such as daily bread, reconciliation with others, and rescue from physical temptation (Luke 11:1–4). Jesus taught that attending to the physical needs of people flows out of the salvation He gives: "'For I was hungry and you gave Me food, I was thirsty and you gave Me drink, I was a stranger and you welcomed Me, I was naked and you

---

10   Ignatius, "Letters of Ignatius: To the Ephesians," trans. Cyril C. Richardson, *Early Christian Fathers*, vol. 1, The Library of Christian Classics (Philadelphia: Westminster Press, 1953), 90, §7.

clothed Me, I was sick and you visited Me, I was in prison and you came to Me'" (Matthew 25:35–36).

Finally, in the final hours of Jesus' earthly ministry, He prayed, "I do not ask that You take them out of the world, but that You keep them from the evil one.... As You sent Me into the world, so I have sent them into the world" (John 17:15, 18). Even as Jesus was departing from this world, He taught His followers that they were being sent into the world to engage it in real and meaningful ways.

CRUCIFIXION

The cross of Christ is a powerful example of God's engagement with the physical realm. Real wood composed the cross on which Jesus was crucified. That wood—perhaps dogwood, cedar, cypress, or olive—had grown in the ground from the day a germinated seed sprouted. This wood was cut and hewn by a real person. The real nails hammered into Jesus' hands and feet had to be transformed from raw iron ore and wrought into shape in a workshop. Real whips made from leather were thrashed across His skin, and piercing thorns were twisted into a crown and placed on His head. God provided the physical means of suffering for Himself. He enabled His own creation to bring forth the tools of torture on which He would offer Himself.

Just as they had to defend the incarnation, the Early Church also had to defend the reality of Jesus' suffering on the cross. There were numerous attempts to minimize the real pain and blood that was shed by Jesus during His crucifixion. A confused belief known as Docetism arose in the first and second centuries from within the religion of Gnosticism. This confused doctrine claimed that Jesus only *appeared* to be human. He was not actually human, nor did He physically suffer or die on the cross; rather, the crucifixion of Jesus was an apparition or phantasm that seemed to be human flesh and blood. Irenaeus of Antioch clarified the ways in which Docetism was incompatible with the real suffering and blood of the crucifixion: "And how, again, supposing that He was not flesh, but was a man merely in appearance, could He have been crucified, and could blood and water have issued from His pierced side?"[11]

---

11   Irenaeus, "Against Heresies," *Ante-Nicene Fathers*, vol. 1, trans. Alexander Roberts and James Donaldson (New York: Charles Scribner's Sons, 1905), 507.

RESURRECTION

The climactic center of God's plan of salvation is the empty tomb of Jesus. This is the nucleus of Scripture and salvation, human history and eternal hope. Everything coalesces around the power of the empty tomb. And it is here that God again confirms the vital importance of the physical realm. The body of Jesus, the same body that gestated in the womb of Mary, finally emerges victorious from the tomb.

There are numerous eyewitness accounts of the resurrection described in the Gospels. These eyewitness accounts do more than simply prove the accuracy of Jesus' prophetic words about the resurrection. They prove that He was physically raised from the dead: "And behold, Jesus met them and said, 'Greetings!' And they came up and took hold of His feet and worshiped Him" (Matthew 28:9). Notice that Matthew reports the disciples taking hold of His feet. This is an important detail in the resurrection of Jesus. In the ancient world, it was commonly believed that spirits and ghosts did not have feet. Since the disciples were holding onto the feet of Jesus, this means they were not clinging to a mere specter or spirit. They were holding real flesh and blood raised from the dead.

From the womb to the empty tomb, the teachings, life, death, and resurrection of the incarnate Jesus prove God's care and concern for the physical world. The Gospels make it clear that God is not only concerned with souls, but also bodies. He does not only engage the spiritual realm, but also the physical. He makes all things new. This means that God's work of salvation in Jesus encompasses the seen and unseen, the spiritual and physical, the eternal and the temporal. Christians believe that following Jesus is not merely a spiritual matter, but also a physical matter.

CHRISTIANITY IS ABOUT BODY AND SOUL, PHYSICAL AND SPIRITUAL

Being a Christian is far from escaping the physical world and tending only to the needs of the soul. This is, however, a frequent caricature of the Christian faith. Our culture assumes that the followers of Jesus long for the day when they can enjoy an eternally disembodied existence in the clouds of heaven. There is an assumption that worship is about transcending the here and now in order to focus on the ethereal presence of God somewhere far away. And many people depict Christians as engaging in spiritual practices that are completely detached from the physical realm; when a natural disaster occurs, Christians retreat into closets to pray while the rest of the world gets busy working on relief efforts. These are all distortions of what it really means to be a follower of Jesus.

HOPE

The fundamental Christian hope is not dying and going to heaven. Death is not the joyful release of the soul from the body, nor is death the ultimate hope of a follower of Jesus. Christians believe death is a curse (Genesis 3:19) and a terrible thing (Psalm 55:4). But Christians believe that on the Last Day, Christ will return to judge the living and the dead (2 Timothy 4:1; 1 Peter 4:1–5; Revelation 20:11–15; see also the Nicene Creed). Christ's resurrection is our hope. His resurrection guarantees our resurrection: "But in fact Christ has been raised from the dead, the firstfruits of those who have fallen asleep.... But each in his own order: Christ the firstfruits, then at His coming those who belong to Christ" (1 Corinthians 15:20, 23). Dying in faith and going to heaven are a penultimate hope; rising to eternal life in the resurrection on the Last Day is our ultimate hope.

The Christian hope is not a salvation only for the soul or a spiritual existence in heavenly clouds. Rather, the Christian hope is for body and soul—a physical and spiritual salvation in Christ Jesus. This means that followers of Jesus refuse to speak Platonic platitudes at a funeral by saying, "That's not really grandpa; that's just his body," or "Death should be a cause for celebration." Instead of dismissing the importance of the body or the curse of death, Christians cling to the resurrection hope depicted in Scripture: "In a moment, in the twinkling of an eye, at the last trumpet. For the trumpet will sound, and the dead will be raised imperishable, and we shall be changed" (1 Corinthians 15:52).

WORSHIP

Christian worship is often misrepresented as a purely spiritual endeavor. Prayers ascend like a roman candle, praise floats into the ether, and God is somewhere up there hopefully listening in to hear His name. If we sing extra loudly and enthusiastically, turn the smoke machine on high, and really get into it this time, then we just might attract God's attention. This is a distortion of Christian worship. It is not about worshipers reaching out to a distant God somewhere in the spiritual realm; worship is about the presence of God dwelling in the midst of His people through Word and Sacrament in a real and tangible way.

Jesus promised to be present when His followers gather together in His name (Matthew 18:20). Beginning worship with the Invocation—"In the name of the Father and of the Son and of the Holy Spirit"—is not an invitation for people to check out and begin composing their grocery list. Rather, the Invocation brings to the forefront the real and meaningful presence of God dwelling in the midst of His people. This presence of God in worship continues throughout the Divine Service. Confession and Absolution is a real interchange between God and His people in the present moment; sins are actually confessed, and the forgiveness of Christ Jesus actually removes ugly, horrific sins. Hearing God's Word in worship is not a mere recitation of antiquated documents. God's Word speaks in the here and now, and it is "sharper than any two-edged sword, piercing to the division of soul and of spirit, of joints and of marrow, and discerning the thoughts and intentions of the heart" (Hebrews 4:12). The bread and wine of Holy Communion and the waters of Baptism are the earthy and tangible means by which God delivers the forgiveness of sins.

From the Invocation to the Benediction, worship is not about ascending into the spiritual realm of God. Rather, the inverse is closer to the truth: worship is about God descending into the physical realm of humanity. Worship is God interacting with us in physical time and space. God's Word touches our eardrums through sound waves; forgiveness enters our bodies when we eat and drink the body and blood of Christ Jesus. The peace God gives through His gifts in worship guard not only our souls but also our hearts and minds unto eternal life.

SACRAMENTS

Jesus gave His followers a tremendous gift when He said, "Take, eat; this is My body. . . . Drink of it, all of you, for this is My blood of the covenant, which is poured out for many for the forgiveness of sins" (Matthew 26:26–28). This meal, celebrated by the followers of Jesus since it was first instituted, is the real presence of Christ Jesus. Holy Communion is the tasteable and touchable, real and physical presence of Jesus. The Lord's Supper is God's grace and mercy made tangible and delectable. Whenever Christians gather together around the Lord's Table, they are defying claims that being a Christian is a strictly spiritual experience.

Baptism is equally physical. It involves water and the Word of God. Baptism is not just a spiritual spritzing; God has commanded that water—hydrogen and oxygen molecules bonded together by unseen forces—be used to deliver His promises. God claims a person as His own through Baptism by placing His name on the individual. Living in the promises of Baptism is an active and ongoing experience. We physically make the sign of the cross often to recall the waters of Baptism and real and present promises of God flowing in our life. The Sacraments are unequivocally spiritual yet undeniably physical.

SANCTIFICATION

The aim of the Christian life is the physical resurrection. Christian worship is the physical experience of God's presence and promises. The Sacraments unite spiritual blessings with physical means. Hopefully, it is becoming apparent that the Christian life is much more than just a spiritual longing to be free from the confines of the physical realm. A fourth example of how Christianity focuses on the physical as well as the spiritual is something called sanctification: the process by which the Holy Spirit makes holy those who believe in Jesus.

The Holy Spirit transforms lives of sin and rebellion in order to bring about holiness and goodness. The Christian life is a heart and mind, body and soul set on the Spirit. This does not mean rejecting the physical world and becoming a spiritual hermit.

There are verses in the Bible, however, that might give the impression that physical things are bad: "For to set the mind on the flesh is death, but to set the mind on the Spirit is life and peace" (Romans 8:6). What does this mean? Does it mean the physical world is bad and the spiritual world is good? No. Rather, the apostle Paul is saying that it is wrong to be led by *only* flesh and blood and the physical world. The word that he uses for "mind"—φρόνημα (pronounced *phronēma*)—is more than just the brain or thoughts. It indicates something like "mind-set" or "aims and aspirations"—what is leading you, or the thing you strive to reach. Paul's words warn against the dangers of following the lead of only our flesh and the physical realm. He warns against blindly following our sinful desires and our bent passions.

Sanctification means refusing to be led by only your heart and soul, flesh and passions. Instead, sanctification means being led by God. Sanctification is about the Spirit of God working in very tangible ways in your life. It is God bringing about spiritual and physical obedience, trust in the promises of Jesus, and an unwavering conviction to follow closely wherever He leads. This includes following Him in the midst of down-and-dirty, real-life experiences: temptations at work, challenges in parenting, and conflicts with hard-to-love individuals.

CHRISTIANITY CARES ABOUT THE EARTH

Because of the confusion about the importance of God's physical creation in Christianity, the Christian faith has also been accused of despising the earth, disregarding environmental issues, and directly causing many modern ecological problems. This notion gained traction in society when a historian named Lynn White Jr. wrote an article entitled "The Historical Roots of Our Ecologic Crisis" in 1967. In this article, White placed the blame of modern environmental issues squarely on Christianity: "We shall continue to have a worsening ecologic crisis until we reject the Christian axiom that nature has no reason for existence save to serve man."[12] White argued in the article that Christianity advocates ruthless dominion over the earth and unfettered dominance over other creatures.

One of the most rampant misunderstandings of Christianity has to do with its relationship to the earth and other creatures. These misunderstandings come from both outside and inside the Christian faith. To be certain, many people outside of Christianity contort Scripture to make it sound like God's creation should be utterly disregarded. Nevertheless, many people within Christianity have also greatly confused the important role that human creatures have in being stewards and caretakers of God's creation. These external and internal misunderstandings have merged together and proclaimed a common message: Christians do not care about the earth.

This sentiment is inaccurate and untrue. Even a brief and surface reading of Scripture makes it clear that human creatures have genuine responsibility to be stewards of God's creation. One of the most commonly misconstrued texts in Scripture is Genesis 1:28: "And God said to them, 'Be fruitful and multiply and fill the earth and subdue it, and have dominion over the fish

---

12   Lynn White Jr., "The Historical Roots of Our Ecologic Crisis," *Science* 155 (March 10, 1967): 1207, http://www.jstor.org/stable/1720120?origin=JSTOR-pdf&seq=1#page_scan_tab_contents.

of the sea and over the birds of the heavens and over every living thing that moves on the earth.'" These words are often confused in two major ways:

Be Fruitful and Multiply: Many people wrongly assume that the command in Genesis 1:28 was given only to God's human creatures. However, God pronounced the same command on the fifth day of creation to other nonhuman creatures: "And God blessed them, saying, 'Be fruitful and multiply and fill the waters in the seas, and let birds multiply on the earth'" (Genesis 1:22). The first time this command was uttered in Scripture, therefore, it was directed to nonhuman creatures, not human creatures. God's desire for His creation to be fruitful and multiply is reiterated multiple times in Genesis (1:28; 8:17; 9:1, 7). It is clear the God's desire for fruitfulness and multiplication is not limited only to human creatures, but rather all living things that God has made.

Have Dominion: The word *dominion* has been tortured and twisted. Both non-Christians and Christians have warped the meaning of this word in Genesis 1:28 into something entirely unrecognizable and detached from the meaning of this word in its other occurrences in the Bible. The charge in Genesis 1:28 to have dominion over other creatures and over the earth has been wrongly turned into uninhibited reign and rule. Elsewhere in Scripture, dominion is depicted as something that is exercised with care and caution. For instance, Leviticus 25:43 says that though one human may have dominion over another, this dominion must always be conducted in light of God's far greater dominion: "You shall not rule over him ruthlessly but shall fear your God." Likewise, as human creatures exercise dominion over the rest of God's creation, they do so with full awareness that they are caring for something that is not their own.

Scripture makes it abundantly clear that God's creation is good—and therefore worthy of our care and protection. Psalm 19 describes how God's creation declares His glory and proclaims His handiwork. Psalm 104 details how all creatures, human and nonhuman, rely on God's sustaining gifts of water and food, shelter and protection. Psalm 148 rhapsodizes on God's creation singing His praises: "Praise Him, all His angels; praise Him, all His hosts! Praise Him, sun and moon, praise Him, all you shining stars! Praise Him, you highest heavens, and you waters above the heavens! Let them praise the name of the LORD! For He commanded and they were created. And He established them forever and ever; He gave a decree, and it shall not pass away" (Psalm 148:2–6).

Just as the whole creation was cursed by the sin of Adam and Eve (Genesis 3:17), the whole creation longs for the undoing of the curse (Romans 8:19–22). God created something very good (Genesis 1:31), and though the world is marred and scarred by sin, He is making all things new in Christ Jesus and has promised to return and finish what He has begun (Revelation 22:20). The Christian faith is misconstrued and misrepresented when it is depicted as loathing the earth and despising other creatures. Similarly, Christians are misguided and mistaken when they act as if caring for God's creation and other creatures is not their responsibility.

CONCLUSION

Christians are not only concerned with spiritual things. People wrongly assume that if something has matter, then it must not matter to the followers of Jesus. The life, death, and resurrection of Jesus are powerful antidotes to this inaccurate claim. In Jesus, God entered into His creation in flesh and blood, embraced life in the physical realm, shed His real human blood on the cross, and rose victorious over death on Easter.

The Christian life is not about escaping the physical realm in order to live a blissfully disembodied existence in heaven. Instead, Christianity is about God loving physical humanity—rather than scorning it—by coming as one of us; Christianity is about heaven coming to earth and God's Spirit transforming our flesh that we have corrupted: "The first man was from the earth, a man of dust; the second man is from heaven. As was the man of dust, so also are those who are of the dust, and as is the man of heaven, so also are those who are of heaven. Just as we have borne the image of the man of dust, we shall also bear the image of the man of heaven" (1 Corinthians 15:47–49). Being Christian is living in a way that reveals how dust and heaven, physical and spiritual, God and humanity have all been beautifully and wonderfully brought together in Christ Jesus.

Clear > Confusion =
EMBRACE CREATION

You could embrace God's creation by roaming the earth to clean up garbage and constantly swat Styrofoam cups out of people's hands. You could save water by never showering, or you could move into an adult treehouse to save the forests. You could do all of this in an effort to live out God's call for us to guard and care for creation.

Or you could care for God's creation in ways that are not so weird.

Embracing creation does not necessarily mean going green or embracing any environmentalist clichés. Rather, there are a number of ways you can live in respect and appreciation for what God has made. Exercising godly dominion and simultaneously protecting God's creation might look like this:

Know the Source: One of the smallest steps toward embracing creation is asking, "Where did this come from?" You can do this with any number of objects; however, the food that you eat may be the best place to start. As you prepare a meal, consider the individual ingredients and from where they came. Think for a moment how that particular food item ended up in your kitchen. It likely came from a grocery store. Prior to the grocery store, the food came from either a food-processing factory or a farm. Prior to the factory or farm, from where did the food come? Perhaps now more than at any other time in human history, there is a very large disconnect between us and the source of our food. This may not seem like a big issue (or at least not a Christian issue). However, it is.

On a practical level, if we have no idea where food comes from or how it is grown, then we will have a very hard time understanding all the agrarian references in Scripture. What is

Jesus talking about when He describes grafting olive branches? (Doesn't He mean graphing olive branches?!?)

There are many other ramifications of not knowing from where our food comes. If we do not know the source of our food, we have no idea how the land, animals, or workers are being treated. You have a far greater chance of knowing that kind of information if you consume food that is locally produced.

Restore What Is Broken: God loves and cares for what He has made. He has demonstrated this love and care by restoring all that is dead and broken through Christ Jesus. God has made all things new through the life, death, and resurrection of Jesus. One way that the followers of Jesus can embody the restorative work of God is by restoring something that is broken. This may sound like a feeble effort; however, it is a clear witness to the world that Christians care about the physical realm.

For instance, restoring an old piece of furniture (rather than sending it to the trash heap) is a powerful picture of God's restorative work. Rather than just buying something new, take something that is badly broken and pour your time and sweat into rebuilding it. Or take a patch of soil that is full of thistles and thorns and transform it into a beautiful garden of flowers and vegetables. These kinds of investments can be powerful testaments to the world that the physical realm matters to the people of God. And on a far greater scale, this is what God has done for us in Christ Jesus and what we look forward to when God will forever make all things new.

Learn Some Names: Knowing someone's name is a powerful thing. A name turns something vague and unknown into something specific and known. When you meet someone new, you often ask for that person's name. Why? Because you have met a lot of humans before; this is a specific human, and you'd like to know more about this one in particular.

In the same way, it is very important for us to know the names of specific creatures and aspects of the land around us. Learn the name of the watershed in which you live. Learn what sort of insects and birds frequent your backyard. Learn the names of your neighbors—human and nonhuman—in an effort to better love your neighbors. Something powerful will happen when you begin learning their names. You will not just give them vague and general concern; instead, you will be able to offer them specific and particular love and concern. It is not an accident that God charged Adam with the task of naming the other creatures: "The man gave names to all livestock and to the birds of the heavens and to every beast of the field" (Genesis 2:20).

Rather than excusing ourselves with clichés and caricatures of caring for creation, consider some small but serious ways in which you can live out God's command to exercise care and responsible dominion for what He has made. In Christ Jesus, God has shown that He is deeply invested in the physical things He has made. As the people of Jesus, we can help clear up our culture's confusion by making it known that we are concerned with the physical realm as much as the spiritual realm.

DISCUSSION QUESTIONS

1. In what ways have you encountered people suggesting that Christians are only preoccupied with spiritual things? How might Christians contribute to this confusion?

2. Christians believe that following Jesus is not merely a spiritual matter, but also a physical matter. Why is it so vital for the followers of Jesus to recognize that Jesus' life, death, and resurrection were physical events? What happens when we neglect the physicality of these events?

3. How do the Sacraments defy the claim that the Christian life is strictly spiritual? How are they unequivocally spiritual yet undeniably physical?

4. How would you respond if someone said to you, "The Bible teaches that humans should have ruthless dominion over the earth and unfettered dominance over other creatures"?

CHAPTER

5

OLD-FASHIONED

Dinosaurs have been extinct for a very long time. Their bones are either buried in the earth or housed in museums. People speak of them only in the past tense. Children read about them safely in their beds knowing that there is no longer the threat of a real dinosaur. Sadly, there is no hope of seeing a living and breathing dinosaur today.

The fact that dinosaurs no longer roam the earth changes how we relate to these creatures. For instance, it is hard to imagine that children would wear dinosaur pajamas and snuggle up with their tyrannosaurus rex stuffed animal if the real thing were breathing hot air on their bedroom windows at night. Children would not gleefully pretend to be dinosaurs in the front yard if velociraptors were hiding in the bushes, salivating at the prospect of eating some yummy little human tater-tots. Since dinosaurs no longer live among us, we now study their remains and imagine what life was like when they were around.

Christianity is often depicted like the dinosaurs: an extinct collection of beliefs that once thrived in a bygone age. According to our culture, Christianity is in the same category as dusty dinosaur bones and fossilized remains. The meteorite of modernity came and destroyed the old-fashioned views once held by Christians. Their outdated beliefs and practices have been buried under heaps of new knowledge and enlightened thinking. They lived and moved and had their being in a premodern world that was nothing like the world today. If there is such a thing as a living and breathing Christian today, then he or she is holding on to an old-fashioned confession that is bound to be extinct within a generation. Surely it will not be long until you can visit a museum and view the bones of a *Christianosaurus*.

The world is half right here: Dinosaurs are deceased. Christianity is not.

Nevertheless, that does not stop people from depicting the Christian faith as being outmoded and old-fashioned. Pop culture portrays Christians as people who are out of touch with the present day, entirely obtuse in relation to everyone else, and inexplicably drawn to weird places like musty churches. Politicians often label Christians as an obstinate voter block committed to resisting all progress and longing for the policies of the past when their morality was imposed on society. The overwhelming consensus on university campuses is that Christianity is a lingering vestige of colonialism and imperialism. Modern families see no need to squeeze an antiquated cultural fossil that only Grandma cares about into their overly full calendars.

Our culture may not go as far as openly calling Christianity an old-fashioned remnant that is bound to be dead and gone in a few years; however, our culture is very comfortable with treating Christianity like a dinosaur stuck in another time and place.

CALLING CHRISTIANS OLD-FASHIONED:
A TIME-HONORED TRADITION

Ironically, depicting Christians as an old-fashioned group of people is itself very old-fashioned. The earliest followers of Jesus were ridiculed for holding on to passé beliefs and practices. Describing Christians as old-fashioned, out of touch, and outmoded goes as far back as the Roman Empire. It may still be fashionable to make fun of Christianity, but it is certainly nothing new.

We know this time-honored tradition of calling Christians old-fashioned goes back at least to the second century. A Greek philosopher named Celsus was one of the first people to label Christianity as a naive, bumpkin belief. Celsus's writing has been preserved through an early Christian theologian named Origen (AD 184/5–253/4). Origen's writings contain many lengthy excerpts in which Celsus derides Christianity, Scripture, and Christ Jesus. For instance, Celsus suggests that the Gospel accounts of Jesus are a farce. He argues that the real story of Jesus is very different from what Christians naively believe:

> [Celsus] accuses Him [Jesus] of having "invented his birth from a virgin," and upbraids Him with being "born in a certain Jewish village, of a poor woman of the country, who gained her subsistence

by spinning, and who was turned out of doors by her husband, a carpenter by trade, because she was convicted of adultery; that after being driven away by her husband, and wandering about for a time, she disgracefully gave birth to Jesus, an illegitimate child, who having hired himself out as a servant in Egypt on account of his poverty, and having there acquired some miraculous powers, on which the Egyptians greatly pride themselves, returned to his own country, highly elated on account of them, and by means of these proclaimed himself a God."[13]

In other words, Celsus argues that Christians hold to an old story that has been disproved a long, long time ago. Celsus intimates that the truth of Jesus is clear to rational people such as himself, yet Christians insisted on clinging to an old-fashioned yarn about Jesus' miraculous birth and claims of divinity.

Similar to Celsus, a third-century philosopher named Porphyry derided Christianity as being composed of backward beliefs that were absurdly out of touch with modern knowledge. According to Eusebius, Porphyry wrote a text against Christians in which he decried the idiocy of Origen believing the antiquated teachings of Christianity even though he had been highly educated:

As an example of this absurdity take a man whom I met when I was young, and who was then greatly celebrated and still is, on account of the writings which he has left. I refer to Origen, who is highly honored by the teachers of these doctrines. . . . But Origen, having been educated as a Greek in Greek literature, went over to the barbarian recklessness. And carrying over the learning which he had obtained, he hawked it about, in his life conducting himself as a Christian.[14]

Porphyry describes Christianity as "barbarian recklessness." Calling someone a barbarian is one of the oldest insults in human history. The word appears to have originated sometime around the Greco-Persian Wars

---

13   Origen, "Against Celsus" 1.28, *Ante-Nicene Fathers*, vol. 4, trans. Alexander Roberts and James Donaldson (Grand Rapids: Eerdmans, 1956), 408.

14   Eusebius, "Church History" 6.19.5–7, *A Select Library of Nicene and Post-Nicene Fathers of the Christian Church*, vol. 1, Philip Schaff and Henry Wace, eds. (Grand Rapids: Eerdmans, 1952) 265–66.

(fifth century BC). It was used to deride anyone who was not Greek. The Romans used the term in a similar way to accuse someone of being uncivilized, backward, primitive, or savage. Calling the Christian faith "barbarian recklessness" is accusing it of being a step in the wrong direction; rather than leading people into the future, Christian beliefs and teachings were leading people into the past and stifling refined culture and knowledge. The fact that Origen had access to Greek education yet still remained a Christian was an absurdity in the mind of Porphyry.

Though the trend of calling Christianity a collection of old-fashioned beliefs and practices began in the Early Church, it grew to a swell in subsequent generations. During the Enlightenment, it became a societal sport to make fun of Christians for being out of touch with the contemporary world. Some of the most cutting insults about Christianity during the Enlightenment came from the French writer Voltaire:

> **May the great God who hears me—a God who certainly could not be born of a girl, nor die on a gibbet, nor be eaten in a morsel of paste, nor have inspired this book with its contradictions, follies, and horrors—may this God, creator of all worlds, have pity on the sect of the Christians who blaspheme him. May he bring them to the holy and natural religion, and shower his blessing on the efforts we make to have him worshipped. Amen.**[15]

Like many others in Europe in the eighteenth century, Voltaire sarcastically mocked traditional Christian beliefs such as Holy Communion, Jesus' incarnation and crucifixion, and the inspiration of Scripture. Many were drawn to rejecting traditional Christian beliefs in favor of natural religion or deism. The basic premise of deism is that there is a God; however, this divine being is entirely uninvolved in the world. Like a watchmaker does not interfere with a watch after it has been made, God supposedly does not interfere with creation in any way. Deism rejected the divinity of Jesus and threw out His incarnation, miracles, and resurrection. It was fashionable to be a deist; it was old-fashioned to be a Christian.

Building on the work of Voltaire and other Enlightenment thinkers, a number of critics in the nineteenth century ridiculed Christianity with even greater vitriol. The German philosopher Friedrich Nietzsche provocatively

---

15   Voltaire, "The Sermon of the Fifty," *Toleration and Other Essays*, trans. Joseph McCabe (New York: G. P. Putnam's Sons, 1912), 182, https://archive.org/details/tolerationother00volt.

declared, "God is dead," by which he meant the need to believe in God was dead and deceased.[16] Nietzsche argued that society no longer needed to believe in God in order to establish morality or values. This led Nietzsche to reject Christianity as a dusty antique from a bygone era:

> **When on a Sunday morning we hear the old bells ringing, we ask ourselves: Is it possible? All this for a Jew crucified two thousand years ago who said he was God's son? The proof of such an assertion is lacking.—Certainly, the Christian religion constitutes in our time a protruding bit of antiquity from very remote ages and that its assertions are still generally believed—although men have become so keen in the scrutiny of claims—constitutes the oldest relic of this inheritance. . . . How ghostly all these things flit before us out of the grave of their primitive antiquity! Is one to believe that such things can still be believed?[17]**

It is, in the words of Nietzsche, unbelievable that people actually believe in Jesus. People have been doing it for thousands of years. Celsus, Porphyry, Voltaire, and Nietzsche are just a few examples of the countless people in history who have dismissed followers of Jesus as being obsolete and passé.

Although it has been happening since the Early Church, people continue to mock Christians as being out of touch with the here and now. Our culture ribs the followers of Jesus for believing that God could make a human life out of a rib. The world laughs when Christians hold on to beliefs that everyone else dismissed a long time ago. At best, people assume that Christians just did not get the memo about how the rest of the world has moved on from this whole Jesus thing. At worst, people vilify Christians as intellectual infants bent on holding society back from making any sort of forward progress.

None of this should come as a surprise. Christians should not be surprised that others mock them as being out of touch, out of step, or out-and-out backward. Jesus made it abundantly clear that following Him will take you

---

16   Friedrich Nietzsche, *The Joyful Wisdom*, trans. Thomas Common, Paul V. Cohn, and Maude D. Petre (Edinburgh; London: T. N. Foulis, 1910), 168, http://www.gutenberg.org/ebooks/52124.

17   Friedrich Nietzsche, *Human, All Too Human: A Book for Free Spirits*, trans. Alexander Harvey (Chicago: Charles H. Kerr and Company, 1908), 149–50, http://www.gutenberg.org/files/38145/38145-h/38145-h.htm.

in a markedly different direction from the rest of the culture. Following Jesus was, is, and always will be countercultural.

TAUNT, FOLLY, AND HATRED

> Jesus came into the world, and everyone—Jews and Gentiles, scribes and Pharisees, rich and poor, and everyone in between—celebrated His arrival. Every word He spoke, every miracle He performed, and every parable He told were well-received by the world. The religious leaders were giddy with excitement to hear Him declare, "But woe to you, scribes and Pharisees, hypocrites! For you shut the kingdom of heaven in people's faces. For you neither enter yourselves nor allow those who would enter to go in" (Matthew 23:13).

Nope. None of that is accurate.

Jesus came into a world of resistance and hostility against Him. He was not yet weaned from His mother when King Herod attempted to kill Him (Matthew 2:13–18). He encountered opposition to His teaching (Mark 12:13; Luke 10:25). He elicited scorn when He healed (Matthew 12:10; Mark 5:17). He was ridiculed, mocked, and dismissed (John 8:48; Matthew 27:27–31; Luke 23:39). Jesus was openly shamed and rejected by those who were in the center of the culture.

Why was Jesus greeted with such disdain and disregard? The kingdom of heaven—the reign and rule of God—had come into the world. This was good news for those who had been awaiting the mercy of God, the coming of the Messiah, and the outpouring of the Spirit. But this was bad news for those who were drunk with pride, power, riches, or self-righteousness: "He has shown strength with His arm; He has scattered the proud in the thoughts of their hearts; He has brought down the mighty from their thrones and exalted those of humble estate; He has filled the hungry with good things, and the rich He has sent away empty" (Luke 1:51–53).

The followers of Jesus should not be at all surprised when the world greets them with insults, condescension, and outright hatred. Jesus taught His followers that others would revile them on account of Him: "Blessed are you when others revile you and persecute you and utter all kinds of evil against you falsely on My account. Rejoice and be glad, for your reward is great in heaven, for so they persecuted the prophets who were before you" (Matthew 5:11–12). Jesus clearly taught that the hatred the world has for Him would be translated into hatred for His followers: "If the world hates you, know that it has hated Me before it hated you. If you were of the world, the world would love you as its own; but because you are not of the world, but I chose you out of the world, therefore the world hates you" (John 15:18–19).

Christianity is a threat to the status quo of this world. The life, death, and resurrection of Jesus has the power and potency to disrupt everything: sin, wealth, privilege, and culture. Those who are in positions of power in the world are often deeply suspicious of Christ Jesus. This is not limited to formal positions of power such as government officials and wealthy business leaders. Rather, anyone who stands to lose power and control is often resistant to the Gospel of Jesus Christ.

We all stand to lose something in Christ Jesus. The Gospel destroys our false self-righteousness, our prideful trust in our own abilities, and our arrogant condescension toward our neighbors. The teaching of Jesus deconstructs our idols, sin, lusty impulses, and spiritual cancer. In Christ Jesus, we stand to lose our illusion of control, power, autonomy, and self-reliance. In the presence of Jesus, we cannot help but join with Simon Peter saying, "Depart from me, for I am a sinful man, O Lord" (Luke 5:8).

Thankfully, He never departs from us. Although sin cries out for Jesus to depart from our presence, He refuses to listen. Jesus has seen it all—our sin, brokenness, mangled motives, and wayward actions—yet still He embraces us with forgiveness and mercy, salvation and redemption. We stand to lose everything in Jesus: sin, pride, ego, judgment, and death. And we stand to gain everything in Jesus: holiness, peace, righteousness, love, and eternal life. The painful yet beautiful truth of the Gospel is that dying to ourselves means living in Jesus.

The world hears all this—gaining by losing, living by dying, strength by weakness—and scoffs. The world agrees with Celsus and Porphyry, assuming that these are mere yarns believed by simpleminded bumpkins.

The world utters a resounding "Amen!" when Voltaire and Nietzsche claim that Christianity is an old-fashioned assemblage of teachings and practices that should have died off generations ago. And yet, all of this simply confirms the Word of God:

> But God chose what is foolish in the world to shame the wise; God chose what is weak in the world to shame the strong; God chose what is low and despised in the world, even things that are not, to bring to nothing things that are, so that no human being might boast in the presence of God. And because of him you are in Christ Jesus, who became to us wisdom from God, righteousness and sanctification and redemption, so that, as it is written, "Let the one who boasts, boast in the Lord." (1 Corinthians 1:27–31)

Parts of Christianity will always be out of step with the world. The cross of Christ will always be associated with folly and foolishness. Therefore, the followers of Jesus might as well embrace the accusations of being outmoded, outdated, and old-fashioned. These accusations have been happening for thousands of years. And they will undoubtedly continue until Christ's return.

LONGING TO BE COOL, EMBRACING ETERNAL RELEVANCE

However, the incessant accusations of being old-fashioned and uncool may lead some Christians to seek out ways of being fashionable and cool. The followers of Jesus, accused of being squares and rubes, may try to counter this claim by seeking out cool pastors, preaching cool sermons, or drinking cool fair-trade coffee. Somewhere within each of us is the deep longing for the culture to pay attention to the followers of Jesus and deem us relevant and cool.

Do you remember the Harlem Shake viral internet meme? Yeah, me neither. There is a good reason why nobody remembers it: it came and went within a month in 2013. This meme—a short video of people doing a crazy and often lewd dance—swelled to tremendous internet popularity. At the height of the video's popularity, over 4,000 new versions of the meme were uploaded to YouTube per day. (This means that a new version of the video was uploaded roughly every twenty seconds.) Frat brothers, sports teams, and office co-workers were the primary groups creating these videos. However, numerous churches and Christian universities also uploaded their own versions of this lewd video. Some of these congregations, even during a worship service, had everyone doing the Harlem Shake in the sanctuary. Why? *Because it was momentarily cool.*

And just as quickly as the Harlem Shake gained viral status, it disappeared somewhere into the internet cloud. It was relevant for a little over a month. And then the world moved on to the next internet meme.

Followers of Jesus do not need to succumb to fleeting attempts to be culturally relevant or cool. Knowing Christ Jesus is eternally relevant. As long as there are death and sin, brokenness and waywardness, guilt and guile, cancers and miscarriages, suffering and despair, the Good News of Jesus will continue to be relevant. Rather than endlessly chasing after the newest cool, Christians embrace the timelessly true and steadfastly salient Word of God. We do not take our cues from the culture; we take our cues from Christ alone.

As we follow Jesus, we will certainly find many occasions in which we can engage the culture without selling out to the culture. For instance, many popular social causes in our culture that seem to be neat, new, and cool have actually been addressed in Scripture long before it was cool. The Christian Church has worked at providing solutions to these problems for generations.

THIRD PLACES

Social spaces that facilitate community building are often referred to as third places. These places are contrasted with the first two places people frequent—home and work. A third place can be any sort of communal gathering location such as a bookstore, pub, barber shop, or coffeehouse. Many trendy stores and companies actually market themselves as third places for people to gather between home and work. These third places, however, are a catalyst for homogenized society. Gathered around a shared political ideology, hobby, or sensibility, third places are typically bastions for "people like us." These communal places are often monochromatic, socially uniform, and composed of very similar people: individuals from the same age, race, and social standing gathered around a common interest. For instance, the majority of Starbucks customers are high-income, educated, and on the go; the company adds new locations, creates marketing campaigns, and orients its product line to this specific customer demographic.

The Christian Church is a third place unlike so many third places in our society. It is composed of young and old, rich and poor, powerful and destitute. And they are all united in Christ. The Church is a multigenerational, multiethnic, multifaceted multitude of people—all gathered together in Jesus. At the beginning of His ministry, Jesus gathered a mixed bag of people to be His followers: fishermen, zealots, tax-collectors, trailblazers, and wallflowers. The Holy Spirit used these diverse disciples to build a multifaceted church. The one Holy Christian Church—also known as the *una sancta*—does not speak just one language, have one shade of skin, or come from just one strata of society. Local congregations, though not always reflecting the full multifaceted nature of the one Holy Christian Church, are places in which very dissimilar people come together in Christ Jesus. The local congregation is a place where the unity of Jesus transcends the disunity of age, zip code, ethnicity, and social standing.

Sustainability

Individuals, communities, and businesses have taken up the cause of sustainable living in recent years. Our culture has begun to ask questions about whether our present pace of production and consumption is sustainable. How long can we continue to work at this pace before everyone in society has a nervous breakdown? How long can we consume, consume, consume before we have overconsumed? Is it healthy for us to have calendars that cram eight days of activities into a week that is only seven days long? These are all questions related to the topic of sustainability.

It's not a new issue; Scripture speaks to sustainable living in a number of ways. The previous chapter discussed how Scripture addresses caring for God's creation. However, God's Word also addresses sustainability through the topic of the Sabbath. Throughout the Bible, God repeatedly instructed His people to set aside one day in the week for worship, rest, and renewal: "Remember the Sabbath day, to keep it holy. Six days you shall labor, and do all your work, but the seventh day is a Sabbath to the LORD your God. On it you shall not do any work, you, or your son, or your daughter, your male servant, or your female servant, or your livestock, or the sojourner who is within your gates" (Exodus 20:8–10). The Sabbath is far more robust than the narrow view of sustainability often depicted in our culture. Society focuses on sustainability for several generations; the Sabbath foreshadows the eternal sustainability God gives us in Christ Jesus. Society is concerned with work-life balance; God offers rest for our weary bodies and souls through the weekly Sabbath rest and the eternal Sabbath rest in Christ Jesus. True sustainability—the eternal kind of sustainability—comes through Christ.

Solidarity

Standing with the oppressed and advocating for vulnerable people is a paragon of modern virtue. Speaking up for those who cannot speak and standing up for those who cannot stand up for themselves is a very popular social issue in our contemporary society.

Christians have been standing with the oppressed for a long, long time. Throughout Scripture, God has charged His people with the task of protecting those who are exploited, downtrodden, or vulnerable: "For the LORD your God is God of gods and Lord of lords, the great, the mighty, and the awesome God, who is not partial and takes no bribe. He executes justice for the fatherless and the widow, and loves the sojourner, giving him food and clothing" (Deuteronomy 10:17–18). The people of God are to be like their God by protecting sojourners (Exodus 22:21; 23:9), the impoverished (Exodus 23:11; James 2:1–7), and the vulnerable (James 1:27; Matthew 25:31–40). Christians have a long history of caring for the sick, protecting children, and helping people in times of need. In the ancient world, it was the followers of Jesus who remained during plagues to provide care for the community. In contemporary times, the followers of Jesus outpace government agencies when it comes to providing relief during a disaster.[18]

CONCLUSION

Being a Christian means that you will be accused of having old-fashioned, outdated, and antiquated beliefs. This is nothing new; it has been happening for thousands of years, and it will undoubtedly continue until Christ's return. Being rejected by the culture is actually an unavoidable part of following Jesus. He was rejected by the world, and He promised that His followers also would be rejected by the same world that hated Him. As Christians,

---

18   Paul Singer, "Faith Groups Provide the Bulk of Disaster Recovery, in Coordination with FEMA," *USA Today*, September 10, 2017, https://www.usatoday.com/story/news/politics/2017/09/10/hurricane-irma-faith-groups-provide-bulk-disaster-recovery-coordination-fema/651007001/.

our response is not coming up with feeble attempts to depict ourselves as relevant to the world. At best, this will make us relevant for a moment and irrelevant all too quickly. At worst, this conveys a message to the world that the Christian faith is an assemblage of dusty dictums that must be dressed up in order to appear timely and relevant.

Instead, Christians cling to the old, old story of the Gospel. Though it is old, it is neither dusty nor detached from contemporary life. The Word of God, the Good News of Jesus Christ, and the counsel of the Holy Spirit are permanently relevant. This is not a fleeting relevancy like a trend on social media or a viral video. Instead of constantly reinventing our theology or image to try to stay hip, we believe new life in Christ, in love for our neighbor, has made us permanently and eternally relevant.

Clear > Confusion =
OWN THE TRUTH

It's hard to keep up with popular social media platforms. In the olden days, it was fairly easy to know which social media platform was the place to be. That is because there were about two of them: Facebook and Myspace. Today, there are more like two hundred social media platforms. And it is almost impossible to determine which one is the most popular since different generations, nationalities, and people groups gravitate toward different platforms.

In many ways, the way the world understands truth has followed this same sort of profusion and fragmentation. There was a time when determining up and down, right and wrong was fairly easy because there were a finite number of worldviews and understandings of truth. Today, however, there are limitless definitions of truth that differ wildly according to generations, nationalities, and people groups.

The people of God have two options in this situation: we can either be paralyzed by the multiplicity of truth claims, or we can clearly and confidently speak truth. Let's do the latter.

Know Truth: The world is pretty convinced that Christianity is an archaic assemblage of old-fashioned beliefs and practices. As discussed in this chapter, this claim is nothing new. The world has pretty well thought this way about Christianity since the time of Christ. It has always been and will always be a temptation for the followers of Jesus to trade God's eternal and unchanging truth for some counterfeit version of truth. Don't fall for it. Instead, seek to know God's truth in Scripture. God has not hidden the truth in the deep recesses of the universe. Nor does God make us wrestle the truth out of the hands of the sphinx. Instead, God has clearly and openly revealed the truth: "The sum of Your word is truth, and every one of Your righteous rules endures forever" (Psalm 119:160). This means that knowing the truth comes from reading, studying, and meditating on God's Word. So Christians should cling to God's Word.

Speak Truth: Knowing truth compels us to speak truth. Yes, the world will view this truth as peculiar and strange. The world will certainly think that this truth is old-fashioned and out of touch with contemporary thought. No, that does not mean we refuse to speak the truth. Be bold in speaking God's truth even if that makes you look old-fashioned or out of touch with society. It is all right to be out of touch with ever-changing definitions of truth. What matters most is being in contact with God's unchanging truth and speaking that truth into a world that desperately needs to hear it: "Therefore, having put away falsehood, let each one of you speak the truth with his neighbor, for we are members one of another" (Ephesians 4:25).

Live Truth: The people of God know truth and speak truth. And the people of God live truth. Actions, it is often said, speak louder than words. Even better is when our words and actions are congruent with one another. It is a powerful combination when we speak the truth of God's love for others and then we actually live the truth of God's love for others. God's truth is clear and obvious to the world when we speak the truth of God's will and then we believe it enough to actually live it out in our own life. Again, as with speaking truth, the world will very likely look at us as if we are from another time or place. Refusing to cohabitate before marriage, choosing to live simply and generously, and inviting others to hold us accountable and free from sin are all ways in which we can live truth according to God's Word.

Living out of step with the culture provides powerful opportunities to proclaim the Gospel. Do not be surprised when people ask you why you believe what you believe or why you live the way you live. However, also do not be surprised when people mock you for believing what you believe or living the way you live. Take heart knowing that the followers of Jesus have always been out of step with the world. According to Jesus, that is how it should be, because the world loves confusion and Jesus brings truth, light, and life.

DISCUSSION QUESTIONS

1. What are some pop-culture examples of Christians being depicted as old-fashioned and out of touch with the world?

2. Ridiculing Christianity as an old-fashioned belief goes back to the Early Church. Why might this be a perennial insult and accusation made against the followers of Jesus?

3. Jesus clearly taught that the hatred the world has for Him would be translated into hatred for His followers. Yet, we are often surprised when we encounter ridicule or insults. Why are we sometimes surprised when the world hates us for following Jesus?

4. Why is it unwise for Christians to chase the newest "cool" in our culture? Why is it wise for us to embrace ways in which God's Word is permanently relevant?

CHAPTER 6

JUDGMENTAL

Sunday morning at a typical church, according to many people unfamiliar with clear Christianity, goes something like this: A group of self-righteous people gather together for worship. They sing songs, listen to Bible readings, and alternate between sitting and standing. Somewhere around the middle of the service, a pastor gets up and gives a long-winded sermon that paints a bleak picture about how bad the world has become, how sinful people are today, and how God hates the [insert name of people group]. After the service, everyone gathers together for coffee and doughnuts in order to discuss how the sermon did a great job of pointing out how truly awful it is that people insist on [insert verb] all the time. Finally, as everyone drives home, they are satisfied to know that at least they are not like all those [insert adjective] people.

If you asked someone with only a vague knowledge of Christianity to describe what a Sunday morning at church looks like, it is very possible the paragraph above is the response you would get. If the person is too polite to actually say these things, then you can at least be certain that he or she is thinking them. There is a widespread assumption in our culture that Christians are judgmental; Christians look down on other people, cast aspersion on the way that others live their lives, and pass judgment on anyone and everyone.

Passing judgment on another person is one of the most egregious crimes in our contemporary culture. According to the tacit rules of modern society, it is impolite, improper, and imprudent to judge another person for his or her actions. We are all familiar with the litany of rebuttals that people give in response to a judgmental comment: "Don't judge me." "Who do you think you are?" "You don't know the whole story." "Get off your high horse."

Given our culture's disdain for judgmental people and the commonly held assumption that Christians are judgmental people, it is no surprise that many people are suspicious of Christians. We could depict this in a logical syllogism:

> **Major Premise:** Nobody likes a judgmental person.
> **Minor Premise:** Christians are judgmental.
> **Conclusion:** I don't think I like Christians.

This is a serious misconception about Christianity. Being judgmental, condescending, and pompous is an aberration of what it means to be clearly Christian. Following Jesus means admitting we are not in a position to judge others. Do we always get this right? No. Not at all. The followers of Jesus often forget that the position of judge has already been filled by someone far more qualified.

JUDGE: THE POSITION HAS ALREADY BEEN FILLED

God is judge. He alone is able to exercise judgment over all things because He alone created all things. Abraham recognized this fundamental role of God when he spoke to God saying, "Far be it from You to do such a thing, to put the righteous to death with the wicked, so that the righteous fare as the wicked! Far be that from You! Shall not the Judge of all the earth do what is just?" (Genesis 18:25). This position—judge of all things—is one of the most basic attributes of God. He made all things. He determined the form, function, and fit of all things. He knows what is truly good and true. God alone is fit to be judge: "The heavens declare His righteousness, for God Himself is judge!" (Psalm 50:6).

This is why Jesus teaches His followers not to judge others. Jesus makes it clear that, despite the many roles and responsibilities we have, the role of divine judge is not one of them: "Judge not, that you be not judged. For with the judgment you pronounce you will be judged, and with the measure you use it will be measured to you" (Matthew 7:1–2). It is simply not our job to judge other people; there is One who is far more competent already filling the position.

Consider the folly of trying to take someone else's job (especially when that other person is far more competent than you). Suppose that you walked into a coffee shop and went behind the counter. *Don't worry, Mr. Barista, I've got this!* You waltz in and shove the guy out of the way. Never mind the fact that he is skilled at what he does and competent in being a barista. You begin taking customers' orders, although you don't recognize the names of the drinks people are ordering, you don't know where anything is, and you don't know how to execute a simple transaction on the cash register. It would take less than five minutes for there to be a long line of angry customers, froth and foam spewing out of every machine, and widespread macchiato mutiny. Taking over for a barista is one thing; taking over for a heart surgeon, airline pilot, or police officer is something entirely different. It would be utterly ridiculous to hastily step in and try to take the job of someone else who is clearly qualified and competent in what he or she is doing.

However, this is what we are doing when we try to judge others. We are essentially telling God, "Hey, I got this! Don't worry. . . . I know what I am doing." When He tells us not to judge, Jesus is telling us to stay in our lane and refrain from trying to take over God's responsibility. God is the judge of all things, and He is really, really good at what He does.

On the contrary, Christians should probably be the least judgmental people around. That is because, as the followers of Jesus, we have become very aware of our own sin and brokenness. The Law—God's will for how we are to live our lives—reveals the discrepancies between how God made us to be and how we actually are. God made us to fear, love, and trust in Him alone; we instead fear, love, and trust the things God has made more than Him. God calls us to lives of sexual purity; we instead indulge our wayward eyes, wandering minds, and wanton hearts. God calls us to never steal and always protect our neighbors' possessions; we instead capitalize on every opportunity to cut a corner, squeeze out a few more resources for ourselves, and pinch another penny. God calls us to put the best construction on our neighbors' words, actions, and ideas; we read the worst into everything, bend the truth, and malign everyone both online and in person. God's Law shows us again and again and again how we are sinners in need of a Savior. The Holy Spirit convicts us of our sin and leads us to repentance.

As Christians, therefore, we out of all people ought to be most aware of our deep brokenness and need for mercy. We have deserved the full weight of God's gavel coming down on us. If we are honest with ourselves, then we admit that we "have been weighed in the balances and found wanting" (Daniel 5:27).

In the ash and rubble of sin's brokenness, God bequeaths and bespeaks the Good News of Jesus Christ. The Gospel declares that we are forgiven on account of Christ's righteousness. This mercy comes despite our sin, despite our disobedience, despite the death we deserve: "For by grace you have been saved through faith. And this is not your own doing; it is the gift of God, not a result of works, so that no one may boast" (Ephesians 2:8–9). There is no room for us to judge because, apart from Christ Jesus, we would all be judged and found guilty of sin and rebellion, waywardness and all kinds of evil. There is no room for boasting in our own righteousness since our salvation is simply by the grace of God. There is no judgment knowing that we ought to be convicted ourselves.

SPEAKING ON BEHALF OF THE JUDGE

God is more than competent to be judge over all the earth. God does, however, employ His people to speak on His behalf. This dual reality is where the confusion arises, for both Christians and non-Christians. We are not the judge. Yet, we speak on behalf of the judge. There are many examples of this throughout Scripture.

One of the most vivid examples of someone speaking on behalf of the judge—yet not serving as the judge himself—is an interchange between David and Nathan. King David had been living a life of reckless abandon: David had engaged in an adulterous relationship with a woman named Bathsheba, he had concocted a scenario in which Bathsheba's husband was sent to the front line of the war as a death sentence, and then David had gone on with life like nothing had happened. God sent a prophet named Nathan to confront David about this unrepented and persistent sin. Nathan told a story to David that sounded eerily similar to what had actually happened; instead of stealing a wife, however, the antagonist in the story stole another man's sheep. David heard the story and was outraged; then Nathan dropped the bomb on him: "Nathan said to David, 'You are the man!'" (2 Samuel 12:7).

Nathan goes on to speak more of God's Word to David. Nathan confronts David about his adultery with Bathsheba and murder of Uriah the Hittite.

Hearing all of this leads David to realize his sin. He says, "I have sinned against the LORD" (2 Samuel 12:13a). Nathan responds to David's confession with more of God's Word: "The LORD also has put away your sin; you shall not die" (2 Samuel 12:13b). Do you notice what is missing from this whole interchange? Nathan's word. Nathan's judgment. Nathan's condemnation. It is entirely absent. This is not about Nathan judging David for what he had done. Nor is this about Nathan speaking his own word of rebuke or sharing his own forgiveness with David. Rather, it is God speaking in and through Nathan to David. Nathan is not doing the judging; Nathan is only speaking on behalf of the Judge.

The Book of Jonah also offers a depiction of someone speaking on behalf of the Judge, God, but in a markedly different way. Unlike Nathan, Jonah does not do the best job of withholding his own judgment. Instead, he subtly assumes God's role and passes his own judgment and condemnation on the people of Nineveh.

God calls Jonah to go to Nineveh in order to call out against the sin and rebellion of the people (Jonah 1:1–2). This is a clear instance in which the Judge sends someone on His behalf to go speak a word of truth. Instead, Jonah takes a detour onto a boat and then into a giant fish. Why did Jonah try to flee from God's commissioning? It turns out he was not thrilled with how God was going to judge the people of Nineveh: "O LORD, is not this what I said when I was yet in my country? That is why I made haste to flee to Tarshish; for I knew that You are a gracious God and merciful, slow to anger and abounding in steadfast love, and relenting from disaster" (Jonah 4:2).

Jonah was sent to Nineveh to speak on behalf of the Judge. Instead, he began judging and condemning the people before he even arrived. Jonah wanted to drop the gavel on them and then drop the mic. He wanted to stroll out of town smiling while the city burned with God's fiery condemnation. The Judge chose otherwise. He showed mercy and patience, forgiveness and graciousness. Unlike Nathan, Jonah was not satisfied speaking on behalf of the Judge; Jonah wanted to be the judge.

These are just two examples among many more in Scripture. The point is that, as the people of God, we do not do the judging. We may be the ones speaking on behalf of the Judge as we share God's Word of truth with others. But it is very difficult for us to be like Nathan and remain free from personal judgment or condescension. It is very easy for us to be like Jonah and let our personal judgment obscure God's grace and mercy.

Condemn vs. Scrutinize

Where the followers of Jesus often have trouble is separating the difference between judging and speaking truth, condemning and scrutinizing. The word that Jesus uses when He tells us not to judge alludes to condemnation or damnation. Our job is not to determine who or what to condemn or damn, judge or hate. On this point, God's Word is very clear:

> **Why do you pass judgment on your brother? Or you, why do you despise your brother? For we will all stand before the judgment seat of God; for it is written, "As I live, says the Lord, every knee shall bow to Me, and every tongue shall confess to God." So then each of us will give an account of himself to God. (Romans 14:10–12)**

Judging others is out of line for the people of God. We all stand before the Judge; we are not judges ourselves. The pronouncement of judgment is not a present diversion for God's people; the pronouncement of judgment is a future event that will happen when Christ returns.

> **Therefore do not pronounce judgment before the time, before the Lord comes, who will bring to light the things now hidden in darkness and will disclose the purposes of the heart. Then each one will receive his commendation from God. (1 Corinthians 4:5)**

This does not, however, mean that followers of Jesus simply refuse to speak truth or to discern right from wrong. There is a difference between judging others and scrutinizing right and wrong. Followers of Jesus, by the power of the Holy Spirit, carefully and prayerfully discern the will of God (Romans 12:2). Christians refuse to take part in that which is unfruitful, sinful, and downright wrong (Ephesians 5:11).

Christians hold other Christians accountable as brothers and sisters in Christ by confronting one another's sins when necessary (Matthew 18:15–20). They speak the truth in love (Ephesians 4:15–16) in order to support one another and grow together as the Body of Christ. This is not judgment or condemnation; this is speaking God's truth to one another in love. This brotherly and sisterly correction is both given and received as part of being in Christ Jesus: "For just as the body is one and has many members, and all the members of the body, though many, are one body, so it is with Christ. . . . If one member suffers, all suffer together; if one member is honored, all rejoice together" (1 Corinthians 12:12, 26).

INSIDE AND OUTSIDE

Scripture makes it clear that God's people are called to be different from the rest of the world. God's will is true for all people—God has given each person a conscience to help guide them in right and wrong (Romans 2:15). But the people of God have been entrusted with making God's will of right and wrong known throughout the world. This was the role of God's Old Testament people, Israel, as they lived among the nations. God called His people out of captivity in Egypt and made them into a holy people, set apart by Him: "You shall be holy to Me, for I the LORD am holy and have separated you from the peoples, that you should be Mine" (Leviticus 20:26). The Pentateuch (Genesis, Exodus, Leviticus, Numbers, and Deuteronomy) details not only the history of God's work in the lives of His people, but also how they were to live lives distinct from others in holiness and purity because they were His people. They were to be distinct from the other nations outside of Israel as a witness to God among the nations.

This distinction is also present in the New Testament. Those who are in Christ Jesus and are part of the Body of Christ have been renewed in heart and mind through faith in Christ Jesus. The old life of sin and death is no more, and the new life of faith has come by the grace of God. Therefore, followers of Jesus are expected to live lives of holiness and purity unlike those who are not followers of Jesus. The apostle Paul makes it clear in his letter to the Church in Corinth that being in the world and being in Christ are categorically different. The people of Jesus are not called to judge the world; however, Christians do have a responsibility to help fellow Christians in discerning right and wrong: "For what have I to do with judging outsiders? Is it not those inside the church whom you are to judge?" (1 Corinthians 5:12). Notice that he makes a distinction about those who are outside and inside. Christians probably should not be all that shocked that someone who doesn't know Jesus lives in unrepentant sin. But they should be shocked and disturbed when a brother or sister in Christ lives in unrepentant sin. Christians do hold other Christians to a higher standard because we are all part of the Body of Christ.

HYPOCRISY

Call it whatever you want: being two-faced, deliberately double-dealing, or acting in a duplicitous way. They all mean the same thing. And they all share something in common: a duality of opposites. Saying one thing and doing another. Acting one way in public but another way in private. Promising in one instance and breaking that promise in another. These are all forms of hypocrisy.

The word *hypocrisy* goes back to ancient Greek. It originally meant something along the lines of "acting" or "pretending." Jesus taught extensively on the topic of hypocrisy. In the same breath as His warning against judging others, Jesus said,

> **Why do you see the speck that is in your brother's eye, but do not notice the log that is in your own eye? Or how can you say to your brother, "Let me take the speck out of your eye," when there is the log in your own eye? You hypocrite, first take the log out of your own eye, and then you will see clearly to take the speck out of your brother's eye. (Matthew 7:3–5)**

Often when Jesus was teaching about hypocrisy, He was directing His words toward the religious people. He warned about the hypocrisy of giving to others in order to receive praise (Matthew 6:2–4), publicly making a show of prayer (Matthew 6:5–6), and following God with nothing more than vapid words and empty actions (Matthew 23). Present-day followers of Jesus must also be mindful of these warnings against hypocrisy. Jesus frequently taught on this issue precisely because it is so easy for us as humans to slip into hypocrisy.

Christians can fall into hypocrisy in countless ways. But there is one common thread: claiming to be a follower of Jesus, yet not actually following Jesus. This could be as simple as failing to embody Jesus' teaching to love our neighbors as ourselves. It may be a Christian chronically missing worship for several weeks. It may be a very public sin like a Christian cheating on his or her spouse, embezzling from an employer, or physically harming someone. Big or small, private or public, any sin is a sort of hypocrisy for the followers of Jesus. If we are being conformed to the image of Jesus, then sin is both incongruent and inconsistent with our new life in Christ.

In this regard, all Christians are hypocrites. That is to say, a life of sin is hypocritical for the people of God.

Being judgmental, casting aspersion on others, and outright condemning sinful people is also hypocritical for Christians. As followers of Jesus, we need to remain ever vigilant so that our words and actions never mock those who are perishing apart from Christ Jesus. Instead of greeting the world with judgment and condemnation, we greet the world with the Good News of Jesus. This Gospel message is the very same message of hope and salvation that has saved us from a life of sin and condemnation. This is the Good News that has taken us from death to life. Since we are all sinners in need of a Savior, judging others for being sinful is hypocrisy. Now that we have come to know the grace of God in Christ Jesus, speaking the Gospel to other sinners is being clearly Christian.

Proclaiming the Gospel is not to be confused with being judgmental. Telling others about Jesus is not the same as telling or implying to others that you are better than they are. However, it may happen that in your speaking of Jesus, someone will take your words as judgment and condemnation.

Sometimes the onus is on the other person: People may hear as judgmental what we say because they think all Christians are judgmental. People may think that you are condemning them when you are merely speaking God's truth. People may wrongly judge you as thinking you are "holier than thou" simply because you profess belief in Jesus. Scripture makes it clear that sinful hearts are hostile to God: "For the mind that is set on the flesh is hostile to God, for it does not submit to God's law; indeed, it cannot" (Romans 8:7). So do not be surprised when telling someone about Jesus is conflated with being judgmental.

Sometimes the onus is on us: We can unwittingly or unintentionally come across as judgmental or condescending. For example, telling someone that he or she is like a dumb, lost sheep might sound a wee bit judgmental (even if it is biblical). Sometimes we come across like we have it all figured out and the other person knows nothing about anything. We can easily stand atop our self-righteousness and look down on the bad choices, mistakes, and inconsistencies of someone else (all the while forgetting that, apart from Jesus, we are lost sheep with our own mountain of bad choices, mistakes, and inconsistences). We do it more than we think. We do it more than we ought.

The topic of hypocrisy is vital for Christians to address. Jesus talked about it. We do it. And other people notice when we do it. However, there actually is hope in all of this.

As I said earlier, hypocrisy is an old term that goes back to the ancient world. It did not always have a negative connotation; rather, hypocrisy used to be associated with acting and theater. It was not a pejorative term; it was a term used to describe acting on stage. Actors would wear a mask and engage in "hypocrisy." Our word *hypocritical* uses this image because when we are hypocritical, it is as if we are putting on a mask and acting a part. We may be able to fool others, but we cannot fool God. He knows the real us. He knows what is behind the mask.

And He loves us nevertheless.

There is hope for hypocrites like us because Jesus loves us despite what is behind the mask of our hypocrisy. Jesus forgives us even after we try to put on a show with our self-righteousness. Jesus enables us to take the mask off, confront our hypocrisy, and be real with ourselves and others. The only hope for hypocrites is Jesus.

CONCLUSION

Our culture assumes that Christians are a bunch of self-righteous people who gather together to cast judgment and aspersion on others—a group of people who meet on Sunday, munch their doughnuts, and gab about how glad they are to not be like the [insert adjective] people.

What people may not realize is that many Christian worship services begin with individuals publicly confessing their sin: "I, a poor miserable sinner, confess unto You all my sins and iniquities with which I have ever offended you" (*LSB*, p. 184). This is not Christians being judgmental; this is Christians recognizing that they have been judgmental. And sinful. And wayward. And hateful. And hypocritical. And everything else.

Christians confess that we are not the Judge. That position has already been filled by One who is far more competent and qualified than we are. Rather, Christians stand before the Judge of all things only because they are clothed in Christ's righteousness. His mercy and salvation cover them. Therefore there is no room for the people of Jesus to judge or condemn— there is only room for them to say what God has said to them.

Clear > Confusion =
BE CHARITABLE

What comes to mind when you hear the word *charitable*? Giving money. Donating something. Pouring soup in a homeless shelter.

What does not come to mind when you hear the word *charitable*? Thinking and speaking positively about other people. Assuming the best in someone else's actions. Defending and protecting someone else's reputation when it is being dragged through the mud.

It is strange that we think charitability has to be a monetary exchange or some grand gesture of helping someone in need. Rather, we can be charitable all day and across all of our interactions if we refuse to bear false witness against our neighbors. We can be charitable in our thinking and speaking without spending a dollar if we simply speak well of others and protect their reputation. This is particularly important in our online interactions, where the reach of slanderous words and accusations can stretch a long way.

Think before You Post: This sounds painfully obvious. And yet it is painfully overlooked in online interactions. It is very easy to bear false witness about others online because that person is not directly in front of us. Social media creates the perfect environment for putting false words in people's mouths and minds. In a "post first, ask questions later" culture, the people of Jesus are called to a higher standard to pause and think about the fallout of their actions. Ask yourself: Am I somehow lying about my neighbor with this post? Am I putting the best construction on this person? Am I being kind in my assessment of this individual?

Digital Encouragement: Social media is an encouragement desert. Everyone is too busy posting about how cute their kids are, how great their dinner is, or how awesome their vacation is going. When everyone else is patting their own backs, why not do the opposite and publicly encourage someone else? Speak a kind word about someone else. Say something constructive about another person. Share your appreciation and respect for someone in your life. You will be amazed by how just a small word of encouragement can make a big impact on someone else.

Defend a Reputation: Online interactions are tricky because it is all public. Someone says something harmful or hurtful, and it is out there for the world to see. This makes it particularly hard to intervene in a situation and defend someone's reputation. However, the best way to handle this is to be discrete and tactful as you defend someone else's reputation. If possible, pick up a phone (interestingly enough, smartphones can actually be used to call people) and call the person who is spreading hurtful words. If a phone call is not possible, use a direct message or personal note to contact the person. It is important to remember that, even in defending someone else's reputation, we must assume the best and be kind toward the person we are rebuking.

Social media is not the most charitable place in the world. In fact, the IRS is more charitable than most digital spaces. But the followers of Jesus can shine His light into these digital spaces by turning against the tide and being charitable in how we think and speak about others. The sharp elbows on social media can be softened with kind hearts and encouraging words.

DISCUSSION QUESTIONS

1. God is judge of all things. Is this attribute of God commonly discussed? In our portrayal of God, is His ability to judge eclipsed by His other attributes (e.g., being all powerful, all knowing, loving, merciful)? If so, why might that be the case?

2. Agree or disagree: Christians should be the least judgmental people around. How does the power of the Law in our own lives keep us from judging others?

3. Why is it so important to distinguish judging others from speaking on behalf of the Judge? What other examples from Scripture depict God's people speaking on behalf of the Judge?

4. How is sin a form of hypocrisy for Christians? What does it mean that the only hope for hypocrites is Jesus?

BRAINLESS

Popular culture depicts Christians like real-life versions of the Scarecrow from the Wizard of Oz: They lack brains. They desire to have brains, but they must helplessly rely on the brains of other people because they don't have brains themselves. As the Wizard of Oz Scarecrow, Christians are portrayed as intellectually challenged, blown around by the weakest argument, and constantly losing their stuffing. Reality shows, documentaries, podcasts, online articles, and numerous other forms of popular media place Christians somewhere between blissfully ignorant and downright stupid. Although our culture is not so brazen (yet) to come out and say it in so many words, followers of Jesus are viewed as those who flop around while lamenting, "If I only had a brain . . . "

Social media is equally caustic in this regard. Facebook posts about Christianity often hint that Christians are driven by fear, dogma, anger, tradition, feelings, hatred, anxiousness . . . really anything but their brains. Twitter contains tweet after tweet that insinuate the antiquated beliefs and practices of Christianity inhibit logical and intellectual progress in society. Social media users often depict the Christian faith as being far from intellectually coherent, reasonable, or sensible.

Contemporary culture thinks that Christianity is largely pathetic. That is, society assumes being a Christian is entirely based on emotions and feelings. The word *pathetic* is built on the Latin root word *pathos*, which means "suffering, emotion, or feeling." Within the ancient discipline of rhetoric, *pathos* is an argument that appeals to the emotions. This is contrasted with *logos* (an appeal to logic) or *ethos* (an appeal to authority). Contemporary culture assumes that Christians are only concerned with pathos and not logos, that Christians are more feelers than thinkers, more emotional than reasonable, and more pathetic than logical.

BRAINLESS FROM THE BEGINNING

The accusation that Christians are intellectually challenged has deep roots in history. Even within the accounts of the New Testament, the earliest followers of Jesus were accused of lacking critical thinking and intelligence.

Athens was a hub of learning and intellectual inquiry in the ancient world. New ideas, new philosophies, and new ways of seeing the world flowed in and out of this seaside town. Paul traveled to Athens (roughly AD 49) and found it to be a place of intellectual curiosity: "Now all the Athenians and the foreigners who lived there would spend their time in nothing except telling or hearing something new" (Acts 17:21). He was up for the challenge of engaging some of the best philosophical brains of the day with the Gospel of Jesus Christ.

So he told them about the life, death, and resurrection of Jesus while using their own gods as proof of their predisposition for desiring religious truth. Some of the Athenians scoffed at him as merely a disciple of a dead teacher: "Some of the Epicurean and Stoic philosophers also conversed with him. And some said, 'What does this babbler wish to say?'" (Acts 17:18). Ironically, both the Epicureans and Stoics were themselves disciples of dead teachers. Later in his interaction with the Athenians, Paul was mocked for thinking that God raised Jesus from the dead: "Now when they heard of the resurrection of the dead, some mocked" (Acts 17:32a). However, some were open-minded enough to actually listen to Paul's thinking: "But others said, 'We will hear you again about this'" (Acts 17:32b). Though his words were met with a mixed reaction, Paul did not shy away from having intellectual conversations about faith. He dove into them. He went out of his way to intellectually engage with the people in Athens.

Christians continued to be accused of possessing limited mental faculties throughout the second and third centuries. Opponents of Christianity railed against it as being a brainless and nonsensical faith.

As Origen describes it, Celsus (whom we mentioned in chapter 5) attacked the veracity of Jesus' miracles as described in the Gospels:

> **[Celsus] immediately compares them [Jesus' cures or His resurrection or the feeding of a multitude with a few loaves] to the tricks**

of jugglers, who profess to do more wonderful things, and to the feats performed by those who have been taught by Egyptians, who in the middle of the market-place, in return for a few obols, will impart the knowledge of their most venerated arts, and will expel demons from men, and dispel diseases, and invoke the souls of heroes, and exhibit expensive banquets, and tables, and dishes, and dainties having no real existence, and who will put in motion, as if alive, what are not really living animals, but which have only the appearance of life. And he asks, "Since, then, these persons can perform such feats, shall we of necessity conclude that they are 'sons of God,' or must we admit that they are the proceedings of wicked men under the influence of an evil spirit?"[19]

According to Celsus, the miracles of Jesus were comparable to the tricks of a juggler. The implication here is that it is plain and obvious to all intellectually competent people that the miracles of Jesus were a farce that happened to trick thousands of gullible people.

Celsus also went after the disciples, arguing that they lacked the education needed to discern the truth. According to Origen, Celsus said, "Jesus having gathered around him ten or eleven persons of notorious character, the very wickedest of tax-gatherers and sailors, fled in company with them from place to place, and obtained his living in a shameful and importunate manner."[20]

The early fourth-century aristocrat Sossianus Hierocles in the Roman Empire argued that Christianity became a popular movement because uneducated fisherman were gullible enough to believe the teaching and supposed miracles of Jesus. Had these early Christians been as discerning and educated as others in the culture, then they would have quickly rejected Jesus as a fraud. Hierocles argued that Christianity came about through uneducated and brainless leaders:

Why then have I mentioned all this? So that the reader can compare our careful and sober judgment in respect to each with the gullibility of the Christians. We do not think a man who performed such deeds to have been a god, but only a man pleasing to the

---

19   Origen, "Against Celsus" 1.68, *Ante-Nicene Fathers*, vol. 4, trans. Alexander Roberts and James Donaldson (Grand Rapids: Eerdmans, 1956), 427.

20   Origen, "Against Celsus" 1.62, *Ante-Nicene Fathers*, 423.

gods; while they are led by a few illusions to declare Jesus a god. . . . [T]he deeds of Jesus have been exaggerated by Peter, Paul, and people of their stripe—liars, yokels, sorcerers.[21]

One of the most stunningly ancient hostile depictions of Christian stupidity is known as the Alexamenos Graffito.

Tracing from "Ancient Rome in the Light of Recent Discoveries" (1898) by Rodolfo Lanciani
Public Domain/Wikimedia Commons

This is a piece of ancient Roman graffiti (dating to about AD 200) that was found on a plaster wall in Rome. This is possibly one of the oldest surviving depictions of Jesus on the cross. It is, however, mocking Jesus and the Christian depicted with Him. The graffiti depicts a young man (presumably named Alexamenos) worshiping a crucified donkey-headed person. The picture includes a Greek inscription that can be translated, "Alexamenos worships [his] God." This ancient graffiti does more than just suggest Christianity is nonsensical—it claims that followers of Jesus are asses for what they believe.

---

21   Hierocles's words are quoted by Eusebius in his work "Reply to Hierocles," in Philostra-
tus, *Apollonius of Tyana, Volume III: Letters of Apollonius. Ancient Testimonia. Eusebius's Reply
to Hierocles*, ed. and trans. Christopher P. Jones, Loeb Classical Library 458, (Cambridge, MA:
Harvard University Press, 2006), 159, §2.2.

HOLDING SOCIETY BACK?

This view of Christianity is not just ancient history. A bevy of modern figures have made similar assertions about Christianity. A movement known as "New Atheism" has grown in notoriety over the last decade. Contrasted with previous forms of atheism, New Atheism sees theistic religion (that is, a belief in God) as a social construct holding society back from forward progress. Previous generations of atheists may have taken a "live and let live" approach to religion; however, New Atheism says that this is imprudent because allowing religion to persist is a threat to society. This loosely organized movement includes high-profile figures such as Richard Dawkins, Christopher Hitchens, Sam Harris, and Daniel Dennett. Collectively, these four figures are known as the "Four Horsemen of Atheism."

The basic tenets of the New Atheism movement include science over religion, the irrationality of theism, and the urgent need to free society from the shackles of religious belief. There is also an "evangelistic" demeanor within this movement. Rather than evangelizing the world with the Good News of Jesus Christ, the New Atheism movement seeks to evangelize the world with the good news of atheism. This movement sees a bright future, unending hope, and even salvation in scientific discovery and human progress.

The assertions of the New Atheism movement, however, crumble under scrutiny. Even a surface-level examination of recent scientific discovery and human progress reveals that they are not entirely good news.

SCIENTIFIC DISCOVERY

One would have to be willfully obstinate not to admit that some recent scientific discoveries have brought some degree of good into the world. Antibiotics, sanitized water, electricity, and transportation are just a few of the improvements to our quality of life afforded to us by modern scientific discoveries. The fact that we do not have a new plague every couple of years is a by-product of science.

On the other hand, the successes of scientific discovery have recently caused a rise in what is known as "scientism." This term describes the notion that science is the only source of real knowledge. Scientism assumes that science and the scientific method are the *only* ways to describe reality and truth. Many people within the New Atheism movement also tend toward scientism.

We must be cautious, though, not to put such a high value on science that we cannot also recognize its drawbacks and negative affects. Recently, we have been hearing about scientists' concern over antibiotic-resistant bacteria; however, there is little to no mention that this problem has arisen because science has enabled the overuse of antibiotics. Many people are concerned with the possibility of climate change; yet, there is little acknowledgment that scientific discovery has created this problem by inventing endless new ways to consume energy. Nuclear war has been a global concern for nearly fifty years; never mind the fact that we created this problem for ourselves through the scientific innovation of nuclear weapons. Nobody can argue that science is all bad; however, nobody can argue that science is all good either.

HUMAN PROGRESS

Riding atop the steam engine of belief in scientific discovery is the notion of human progress. The basic assumption is that each generation stands on the shoulders of the previous generation and peers off a little further into the realm of progress. The concept of human progress claims that we today are better, know more, and have progressed further than anyone else in human history. And without religion impeding the path forward, humans will continue to venture forward into the great expanse of progress.

A brief glace at headlines, though, should make us hard-pressed to believe unfettered human progress is taking place. It appears that humanity is only making progress in more terrorism, more racism, more mass violence, and more broken families. Human reason has arguably been at the helm of the Western world since the Enlightenment; however, in the last three hundred years we have only managed to progress further into chaos.

Contrary to the claims of New Atheism that Christianity is holding society back, there are extensive examples of exactly the opposite. There are countless followers of Jesus throughout history who have helped to make tremendous strides for humanity in many different disciplines:

PHILOSOPHY

Many foundational figures in philosophy were Christians. Anselm of Canterbury (1033–109) developed a complex argument to prove God's existence. Known as the ontological argument for the existence of God, Anselm used a series of logical statements to prove that God's existence is more tenable than God's nonexistence. Subsequent generations of philosophers have relied on Anselm's work to formulate other ontological arguments; this sort of philosophical argument has become a perennial topic within the discipline and continues to generate discussion for modern philosophers. Thomas Aquinas (ca. 1225–74) is another hugely influential figure within the discipline of philosophy. Aquinas wrote several commentaries on Aristotle's work and helped build the foundation for modern discussions of ethics. Soren Kierkegaard (1813–55), a Danish Christian, founded existential philosophy. That tradition continues to be hugely influential in modern philosophy. Another Christian philosopher, Edmund Husserl (1859–1938), baptized into the Lutheran Church as an adult, is credited with formulating the philosophical study of phenomenology. Phenomenology is used extensively today in modern academia across many different fields.

LITERATURE

Christians have played a hugely influential role in literature throughout the generations. Augustine (AD 354–430), a North African convert to Christianity, helped to develop many concepts within the field of rhetoric. His influence remains as his work is still standard reading for anyone studying rhetoric. Dante (ca. 1263–1321), an Italian Christian, penned one of the most highly regarded works in world literature. His *Divine Comedy* has indelibly shaped how humans think about literature. Fyodor Dostoyevsky (1821–81), a Russian Christian, greatly contributed to both modern literature and modern psychology through his novels *Crime and Punishment* and *The Brothers Karamazov*. J. R. R. Tolkien (1892–1973) wrote several powerful works of fantasy including *The Hobbit* and *The Lord of the Rings*. Tolkien was a faithful follower of Jesus and very influential in C. S. Lewis's conversion from atheism to Christianity. C. S. Lewis (1898–1963) wrote the hugely popular fantasy series The Chronicles of Narnia. Both Tolkien and Lewis wrote allegorical literature that depicted Christianity through fantasy writing.

MATH

A number of Christians have contributed to the field of mathematics. Lewis Carroll (1832–98), a mathematician, logician, and lifelong Christian, wrote *Alice's Adventures in Wonderland* as a way to teach logic. He is also known for writing a number of mathematical works in addition to literary works. Kurt Gödel (1906–78) was a Christian mathematician who was highly respected by Albert Einstein. As a baptized Lutheran and faithful reader of Scripture, he elaborated Anselm of Canterbury's ontological proof for the existence of God. This mathematical version of the argument is known as Gödel's ontological proof. John Lennox (b. 1943) is a mathematician at the University of Oxford, author of over seventy published mathematical papers, and notable Christian apologist. He has on numerous occasions offered rebuttals to the New Atheism movement.

ART AND MUSIC

Both art and classical music are interwoven with numerous Christian composers, artists, and musicians. Michelangelo (1475–1564), Leonardo da Vinci (1452–1519), and Caravaggio (1571–1610) created masterful works of art based on Scripture. Johann Sebastian Bach (1685–1750), Georg Friedrich Handel (1685–1759), and Wolfgang Amadeus Mozart (1756–91) were inspired by their Christian faith to compose some of the most beautiful compositions the world has ever heard. Many of the greatest artistic and musical masterpieces have arisen in and through Christianity.

SCIENCE

There is a persistent myth that the Christian faith is antithetical or even hostile to scientific inquiry. The long litany of Christians engaged in the sciences throughout the generations make this myth untenable. Roger Bacon (1219–92), a Franciscan friar and scholar at Oxford, was instrumental in developing the modern concept of the scientific method. Jean Buridan (ca. 1295–ca. 1358), a French priest and scientist, developed the concept of impetus, which laid the foundation for inertia and eventually the Copernican Revolution. Robert Boyle (1627–91), both a theologian and chemist, is regarded as the first modern chemist and the founder of modern chemistry. The modern science of genetics is indebted to the groundbreaking work of the Augustinian abbot Gregor Mendel (1822–84). And in the last one hundred years, there have been over twenty Christian Nobel Prize Laureates in the sciences (physics, chemistry, medicine).[22]

> **The point is this:** New Atheism's claim that Christians are holding back human progress is nonsensical, untenable, and historically naive. If one were to remove all the contributions made to humanity by Christians, there would be cavernous voids in philosophy, literature, mathematics, art, music, and science.

In other words, there would be a gaping hole in humanity.

LEAN IN AND LEARN APOLOGETICS

As we said, there is a widespread assumption that Christians are brainless believers simply riding an emotional wave of blind faith. This assumption has persisted for thousands of years and many generations. Being a Christian does not require being illogical or insane. But it *would* be delusional for Christians to think that a few well-developed arguments, a couple of quick proofs, or an hour-long debate will suddenly convince our culture that following Jesus is reasonable. We must always remember that God's work of salvation on the cross is considered foolishness by many: "For the word of the cross is folly to those who are perishing, but to us who are being saved it is the power of God" (1 Corinthians 1:18).

Does this mean that we should just roll over and play dead like a passel of opossums? When society accuses us of being brainless, should we confirm their suspicions by utterly lacking the ability to formulate a rebuttal? No. As the people of Jesus, we are to always be "prepared to make a defense to anyone who asks you for a reason for the hope that is in you" (1 Peter 3:15a). This well-known Bible verse is the basis for Christian apologetics. As I mentioned in chapter 1, our word *apologetics* derives from the Greek word for the defendant's rebuttal or response to the accusations made by the prosecution in the classical Greek legal system (ἀπολογία, *apologia*).

---

22   Baruch A. Shalev, *100 Years of Nobel Prizes*, second edition (Los Angeles: The Americas Group, 2003), 57.

Therefore, Christian apologetics is simply providing a rejoinder or response to accusations made against Christianity—it is not trying to force people into the Christian faith through logic.

God tells us to be ready to respond and prepared to defend the veracity of our hope in Christ Jesus. Notice, however, that this verse does not limit our defense to intellectual argumentation. Rather, it also calls us to engage in apologetics through a living defense: "Yet do it with gentleness and respect, having a good conscience, so that, when you are slandered, those who revile your good behavior in Christ may be put to shame" (1 Peter 3:15b–16). The emphasis is on our actions, behaviors, and overall lifestyle.

Apologetics, therefore, is both a *thinking defense* and a *living defense* for the hope that we have in Christ Jesus:

THINKING DEFENSE

This is what most often comes to mind when we think of apologetics. Proofs, theorems, and studies are all examples of this sort of apologetics. In this realm, Christians rely on reason, logic, science, history, archeology, and numerous other resources to build a case for the credibility of their faith. Similar to legal defenses in the court of law, developing a thinking defense for the Christian faith can take many different shapes:

Evidence: Apologetics deals with the viability and credibility of evidence surrounding the Christian faith. Historical corroboration for the biblical accounts, the reliability of ancient biblical manuscripts, and the overall reliability of Scripture are aspects of the evidential case for Christianity. This kind of evidence can also come from extrabiblical accounts of ancient historians and physical artifacts preserved from antiquity up to the present day.

Witnesses: Just as witness testimony is vital in the court of law, apologetics engages the eyewitness testimonies of the followers of Jesus. The well-known apologist Dr. Paul Maier has frequently used this phrase: *myths do not make martyrs*. This phrase captures the power of this eyewitness testimony. Nearly all the disciples died a martyr's death. Had they concocted the story about the resurrection of Jesus, it is highly unlikely that they would all willingly die for a fabricated lie. The hundreds of eyewitnesses to the resurrection of Jesus serve as a powerful defense against claims that it never happened.

Experts: The court of law often calls experts to the stand. In the same manner, apologetics defends the tenability of the Christian faith by calling on various experts. These experts tend to possess a credibility that is widely recognized both within Christianity and outside in the broader community. Some well-known apologetics experts include Justin Martyr, Augustine of Hippo, G. K. Chesterton, and C. S. Lewis. These apologists, having converted from either another religion or atheism, are credible voices outside the Christian community.

More important than knowing any of these aspects of a thinking defense—evidence, witnesses, or experts—is simply knowing God's Word of truth in Scripture. If Christians do not know what they believe, then any sort of thinking defense is bound to crumble. It is vitally important that we have brains filled with God's wisdom, truth, and knowledge in Scripture. The world already suspects that we are brainless believers; if we try to defend the faith without knowing the basics of Scripture, then we will undoubtedly confirm that suspicion for them.

LIVING DEFENSE

An often-overlooked form of apologetics—but also a very important one according to 1 Peter 3:15–16—is the living defense. This apologetic is not focused on intellectual argumentation or debating accusations; instead, this apologetic focuses on living a life that is above reproach, full of compassion, and entirely Christlike. It is about defending the faith with deeds rather than words. This apologetic embodies Paul's words in Romans: "Bless those who persecute you; bless and do not curse them. Rejoice with those who rejoice, weep with those who weep. Live in harmony with one another. Do not be haughty, but associate with the lowly. Never be wise in your own sight. . . . Do not be overcome by evil, but overcome evil with good" (Romans 12:14–16, 21).

This apologetic tactic was employed by a number of early Christians. As increasing numbers of Christians faced persecution in the second and third centuries, many people defended the faith in this way. One such defense is preserved in the Letter to Diognetus—a letter from an unknown author to an unknown recipient. However, scholars estimate that it dates to AD 130–200 and represents one of the earliest known examples of extrabiblical apologetics. The author defends the Christian faith on the basis of how the followers of Jesus live their lives:

> **They obey the established laws, but in their own lives they go far beyond what the laws require. They love all men, and by all men are persecuted. They are unknown, and still they are condemned; they are put to death, and yet they are brought to life. They are poor, and yet they make many rich; they are completely destitute, and yet they enjoy complete abundance. They are dishonored, and in their very dishonor are glorified; they are defamed, and are vindicated. They are reviled, and yet they bless; when they are affronted, they still pay due respect. When they do good, they are punished as evildoers; undergoing punishment, they rejoice because they are brought to life. They are treated by the Jews as foreigners and enemies, and are hunted down by the Greeks; and all the time those who hate them find it impossible to justify their enmity.[23]**

This powerful defense echoes the words of Scripture (namely, 2 Corinthians 6:3–10). The point, both from Scripture and extrabiblical accounts from the Early Church, is that a defense for the Christian faith can be made simply by how the followers of Jesus live their lives. While everyone else knifes one another in the back, the followers of Jesus turn the other cheek. While everyone else suffers from broken marriages and families, the people of God have thriving relationships and a strong family life. While fear and anxiety clench their sharp teeth deeper and deeper into society, Christians live a life of peace and quiet contentment. When everything else is crumbling, the children of God stand firm.

When the world accuses us of being brainless, we show the world that we are neither lacking brains nor hearts. Living a Christlike life is a time-honored and powerful apologetic.

CONCLUSION

Brainless, intellectually incompetent, and obstinately standing in the way of human progress—these are just a few of the many accusations set

---

23   Eugene R. Fairweather, trans., "Letter to Diognetus," *Early Christian Fathers*, vol. 1, The Library of Christian Classics (Philadelphia: Westminster Press, 1953), 217, 5.10–17.

against the followers of Jesus. It is hurtful and mean-spirited. Yet, it is nothing new.

We can play dead and do nothing. We can get upset and hurl insults back. Or we can use both our brains and our hearts to defend the faith.

God gives us all we need to offer this defense. He renews our hearts in Christ Jesus, removing the old heart of sin and anger and giving us a new heart of love and compassion. He renews our minds and fills us with true knowledge and wisdom. He speaks to us through His Word and strengthens us with the Holy Spirit, who counsels our hearts and minds. God has always provided His people with all they need to defend their hope in Jesus and to proclaim the Good News to a world that desperately needs it. He has given you a brain and a heart . . . so use them.

Clear > Confusion =
LEARN APOLOGETICS

The internet is full of listicles and short articles proving the truth and reliability of the Christian faith. Some of these apologetics articles are helpful and accurate; many of these articles are neither helpful nor accurate. One of the biggest mistakes that the followers of Jesus can make is assuming that simply skimming an article of unknown provenance on your phone means you are competent to speak on a particular subject.

What will inevitably happen is this: Armed with your five minutes of reading, you will engage in a conversation with someone and begin using the information you gathered from the article you hastily skimmed. The other person, unbeknownst to you, is extremely knowledgeable in the subject matter being discussed. And you end up looking like a dope for thinking you knew more than you did. (I know this because I have done this myself.)

In order to avoid these embarrassing—and even detrimental—interactions, it is important for the people of Jesus to take apologetics seriously. There are a number of ways in which we can learn apologetics:

Read Expansively: It is vital that we are well read and knowledgeable on a topic. This means that we first and foremost know what we believe and why we believe it. The people of Jesus must be well read in Scripture and the historical confessions of the Christian Church. However, it is important for us to also read both classic and contemporary apologetics books. Still, we cannot stop there. Part of reading expansively means reading the books and writings that are arguing *against* Christianity. By reading the accusations and arguments that people are making against the Christian faith, you will be better prepared to engage these topics when they happen in daily conversation. It will not suffice to hear about these books and authors secondhand from Christian apologists; rather, consider engaging these writings and arguments directly. It may be wise to do so with some fellow brothers and sisters in Christ so that together you can wrestle with these writings.

Go Deep: It is unrealistic and overzealous to think that you can be a competent apologist in all areas. Being knowledgeable about the depth and breadth of many different subject matters is impossible. Rather, consider going deep in one particular area. Dig in to creation studies, the reliability of Scripture, or logical arguments for the existence of God. Not all of these; just one. A mark of wisdom is knowing what you know and knowing what you do not know. Go deep in one area of apologetics so that you can speak boldly and confidently in that subject area. And then be careful and cautious when dealing with a subject area of apologetics that is not your expertise.

Be Nice: This is not exactly in the realm of learning apologetics. Nevertheless, it is an important characteristic that should be maintained throughout all of our interactions with apologetics. The followers of Jesus must be winsome and kind as they defend the faith. Loving your neighbor does not mean arguing him into sheer frustration and anger. If you sense the conversation is getting heated, then come back to it at another time. If you notice people are reporting you online or unfriending you, then consider how tactful and kind you are being in your approach. Defending the faith is not a license to throw verbal rocks at people.

Learning apologetics is hard. Assuming that it is an easy endeavor will inevitably disappoint you or lead you into an embarrassing situation. Instead of thinking so little of apologetics that we assume a five-minute listicle is sufficient, let's think enough of apologetics to lean in and learn more of what we need to know in order to defend our faith and our trust in Christ Jesus.

DISCUSSION QUESTIONS

1. Contemporary culture assumes that Christians are only concerned with feeling and not thinking. Have you ever encountered someone holding to this belief? How did that person depict the Christian faith?

2. The Book of Acts described how some people in Athens mocked Paul as a brainless babbler. Why is it important to realize that some of the people in Athens wanted to know more? How does this encourage our Gospel proclamation today?

3. How is New Atheism distinct from previous forms of atheism? What are some basic tenets of this movement? What are some issues or flaws in the claims of New Atheism?

4. In apologetics, what is the difference between a thinking defense and a living defense? Why is it vital for Christians to engage in both forms of apologetics?

HAPPINESS

*Life, Liberty and the
pursuit of Happiness.*

—DECLARATION OF INDEPENDENCE

These three unalienable rights are described in the United States Declaration of Independence. The full sentence reads, "We hold these truths to be self-evident, that all men are created equal, that they are endowed by their Creator with certain unalienable Rights, that among these are Life, Liberty and the pursuit of Happiness." Thomas Jefferson initially wrote this sentence in the Declaration of Independence differently; his original rough draft described life, liberty, and the pursuit of happiness as deriving from human equality. However, a group known as the Committee of Five was given the task of editing Jefferson's draft. They changed the sentence so that life, liberty, and the pursuit of happiness were divinely endowed rights.[24]

This may seem like a minor editorial change. It wasn't. This change implied a straight line between God and happiness. One of the most foundational documents in American history hints that God desires nothing more than human happiness.

American Christianity has been conflated with the pursuit of happiness. Our culture often thinks that followers of Jesus are pursuing a life of happiness, sunshine, and smiley faces. Jesus will make you feel good about yourself. Churches are like support groups with organ music in the background. And the Bible is chock-full of saccharine platitudes.

---

24   See "Declaration of Independence: Making Comparisons" at https://www.loc.gov/teachers/ classroommaterials/lessons/declaration/pdf/comparisons.pdf.

To be certain, the United States Declaration of Independence did not cause this confusion. It did, however, pave the way in the United States for the Christian life to be confused with a life of happiness.

THE GOLDEN CALF OF HAPPINESS

Few things in contemporary culture are more sacred than happiness. We have developed a number of mantras to reinforce the centrality of happiness in our lives: *"Do what makes you happy." "Find someone who makes you happy." "Don't let anything steal your happiness." "Choose happiness."* Spouses leave one another because they are not happy. Parents pull children out of activities because they are not making them happy. An individual chooses a career solely on the basis of doing what makes him or her happy. Our culture has a canine appetite for happiness. We crave it. We long for it. We worship it. We pursue it.

And it pursues us. Advertisements hawk new products that will finally give us the happiness we deserve—*use this toothpaste and suddenly you will not be so socially awkward.* Marketing agencies spend millions of dollars to convince you that products and experiences will make you happy—*you haven't truly lived until you've taken a motorized wheelchair to the Grand Canyon.* Commercials give you a glimpse at what your life might be like if you buy what they are selling—*your family will have happiness coming out of their eyeballs if you purchase these crescent rolls.* Happiness doggedly pursues us.

And it eludes us. Searching for happiness by purchasing products or experiences never fully satiates our appetite. If anything, it just whets our desire for happiness all the more.

We also frequently turn to social media in our pursuit of happiness. People spend time on social media because they are searching for happiness through community and personal connection with others. We snap, scroll, and tweet hoping that perhaps people, instead of products, will make us happy. The trouble with social media is that, through it, we encounter an endless supply of happier people. Everyone looks prettier, does cooler stuff, and seems more put together than us. People on social media have bigger houses, cuter children, nicer spouses, and generally better lives than we do.

There are numerous studies indicating that the more time spent engaging social media, the more we experience decreased happiness and well-being.[25]

Since real and sustained happiness eludes us, people then often turn to spirituality or religion to find happiness.

> I haven't found happiness anywhere else, so perhaps Jesus can help me. Finding a church will help me to be happy. Perhaps reading the Bible will solve my problems and make me feel better about my life.

These statements are not entirely wrong. There is, without a doubt, real and sustained happiness in Christ Jesus. But here's where the confusion comes in: what is real happiness?

THE BLACK DEATH AND THE *DANSE MACABRE*

Before answering that question, "What is real happiness?" let's turn to the Black Death. (If you weren't happy before, you'll definitely be happy now!) In the Middle Ages, plagues were a horrific and persistent part of life. The worst of these plagues was the Black Death, which spread through Europe in the years 1346–53. While it is hard to determine an exact figure, historians estimate that the Black Death killed somewhere between 75 million and 200 million people. Roughly half of Europe's population at the time died of this pandemic.

The *Danse Macabre* (Dance of Death) became a popular artistic trope in the Late Middle Ages as death was waltzing through Europe. Skeletons and other symbols of death were commonly depicted in paintings and artwork during this historical period. And there was a reason for this recurring emblem of death: it was a daily reality. Entire families could be fine one day and then gone within a week. The ever-present reality of death put

---

25   Ethan Kross et al., "Facebook Use Predicts Declines in Subjective Well-Being in Young Adults," *PLoS One* 8.8, August 14, 2013, http://journals.plos.org/plosone/article?id=10.1371/journal.pone.0069841. doi: 10.1371/journal.pone.0069841. See also Moira Burke and Robert E. Kraut, "The Relationship between Facebook Use and Well-Being Depends on Communication Type and Tie Strength," *Journal of Computer-Mediated Communication* 21.4 (July 2016): 265–81, accessed February 2, 2018, http://onlinelibrary.wiley.com/doi/10.1111/jcc4.12162/epdf.

the topic of justification—that is, being in right relationship with God—at the forefront of people's minds. Since death was a daily reality, people in the Middle Ages were keenly focused on their standing before God. *Am I forgiven? Am I saved? Will God deem me righteous?* These were standard questions and concerns during that time in history.

In a world like that, Christianity was not about being happy or feeling good. Instead, much of the Christian life was directed at dying well. The *ars moriendi* (The Art of Dying) was a central focus of pastoral care in the Middle Ages. Pastoral care was about helping people live with the reality of death, approaching death with resolute hope in Christ Jesus, and awaiting the resurrection of the dead and the life of the world to come. Being happy was, at most, an afterthought in the Christian life, if it was thought of at all at that time. Taking hold of eternal life in the midst of death was at the forefront of premodern spirituality: "For we who live are always being given over to death for Jesus' sake, so that the life of Jesus also may be manifested in our mortal flesh. So death is at work in us, but life in you" (2 Corinthians 4:11–12).

TEMPORAL SECURITY AND THE CONFUSION OF HAPPINESS

The world has changed dramatically since then. Global pandemics are not a fixture of daily life in the modern world. The last five hundred years have witnessed steady improvements in life expectancy. Along with the improvements in life expectancy and health, there have been widespread advances in standards of living in many parts of the world. Death, while it happens every day, is not a daily fear for many people in modern industrialized nations. The vast majority of people in developed nations begin each week assuming that they will survive to see the weekend. This deferment of death has transformed how people approach life.

Fear of death and God's judgment is a back-burner issue for many people in modern society. Fear of meaninglessness and unhappiness, however, is an urgent matter for many people. We look to the judgments of others in our community and on social media to determine how our life stacks up. Rather than awaiting the Last Day when God will judge all things, we look to the daily judgments of others to help us determine whether we are happy and fulfilled. Collecting "Likes" and "Favorites" helps to confirm that we are living right and finding contentment. Being in right relationship with God and prepared for death is something that can wait for another day or maybe never; being happy and in right relationship with the world around us have become the most important goals—and they are urgent matters. Taking hold of your best life now, realizing your dreams, and pursuing happiness are central to many modern understandings of spirituality.

Expecting the Christian faith to be a bastion of happiness is problematic. Jesus never promised that following Him would lead to a life of happiness. Jesus often depicted discipleship as being gritty, challenging, and rigorous:

> **As they were going along the road, someone said to Him, "I will follow You wherever You go." And Jesus said to him, "Foxes have holes, and birds of the air have nests, but the Son of Man has nowhere to lay His head." To another He said, "Follow Me." But he said, "Lord, let me first go and bury my father." And Jesus said to him, "Leave the dead to bury their own dead. But as for you, go and proclaim the kingdom of God." Yet another said, "I will follow You, Lord, but let me first say farewell to those at my home." Jesus said to him, "No one who puts his hand to the plow and looks back is fit for the kingdom of God." (Luke 9:57–62)**

Following Jesus means dying to yourself and living in Him: "If anyone would come after Me, let him deny himself and take up his cross and follow Me" (Mark 8:34). Following Jesus leads to persecution (Matthew 5:10–12; John 15:20). Being a disciple of Jesus is an adventure that stretches our natural comfort zones (Matthew 14:13–21; 17:1–8).

This turns modern conceptions of happiness upside down. "The happy life" in our world is often depicted as a life of personal and spiritual freedom in which one is able to pursue whatever one wants: charting your own course, chasing down your dreams, and taking hold of whatever seems good to you. Happiness is understood as never having to go without, never having to suffer pain or discomfort; happiness is never having to do something you don't want to do. Real happiness, as Jesus describes it, is totally different. It is about dying to ourselves and receiving new life in Christ Jesus. It is obedience to God's will, no matter what it costs us, not obedience to our inner passions and desires. It is dependence on Him in all things and for all things, not independence and autonomy to pursue whatever we want.

Eternally sustainable and truly authentic happiness can only occur under the reign and rule of God.

Being happy, at least as it is depicted in Scripture, is not something that we get to grab for ourselves. Nor is happiness something that we get to personally define or determine. Biblical happiness is defined by God, given by God, and sustained by God. Happiness is not something to pursue; happiness is something God provides.

THE KINGDOM OF HEAVEN
– MORE THAN DELAYED HAPPINESS –

Heaven is often thought of as the place you go when you die. A common misconception about the Christian life is that it trades happiness now for a greater happiness later: Follow the rules and don't have any fun in this life because you will have all kinds of fun and happiness in heaven. Heaven will be a place of free golf and endless steak dinners, and everything will be wrapped in bacon. Just deny yourself now, and you will get to be happy then.

Waiting for heaven is a confusion about Christianity. The Bible does not refer to heaven as merely the place you go when you die. A far more accurate understanding of heaven is the present reign and rule of God. Wherever God is presently reigning and ruling, then that is heaven. This means that heaven can and does come to earth—now. For instance, early in His ministry Jesus proclaimed, "Repent, for the kingdom of heaven is at hand" (Matthew 4:17). Heaven had come to earth through Jesus. The reign and rule of God was present in His teaching and ministry. Similarly, Jesus taught His disciples to pray saying, "Your kingdom come, Your will be done, on earth as it is in heaven" (Matthew 6:10). Jesus desired the kingdom of God in heaven to come and be done on earth—now. Not someday when we die. Not at a future date that is TBD. Jesus taught us that God's kingdom can and does come into the here and now, on earth as it is in heaven. Jesus sent His disciples and told them, "And proclaim as you go, saying, 'The kingdom of heaven is at hand'" (Matthew 10:7).

The happiness of heaven is not merely a future promise. Being a Christian is more than the delayed happiness that will one day occur when we are in the kingdom of heaven. Through faith in Christ Jesus, that day has already arrived. Knowing Jesus and being His disciples means knowing His happiness—as He defines it—today:

Life: Jesus gives life. This is more than just a beating heart and breath in your lungs. The life that Jesus gives surpasses mere bodily life. This is far more than physiological life, but also spiritual life now and forever: "I came that they may have life and have it abundantly" (John 10:10). The life, death, and resurrection of Jesus give us real, authentic, and eternal life because He restores us to what we were created to be and puts us into the relationship with God that we were always supposed to have. There is no greater happiness than the complete and total new life that is ours in Christ Jesus.

Peace: The peace of Jesus is wholeness, completeness, and fullness. The peace of Jesus is not always the absence of war, hostility, anger, or violence; He told His followers that they would encounter hostility and persecution simply for being His disciples. However, the peace of Jesus is the presence of divine peace, meaningfulness, and satisfaction. The Hebrew word for this peace of God is *shalom*. It is the peace of a calmed storm (Mark 4:39), the peace of healing (Mark 5:34), and the peace of eternal safety (Psalm 4:8). Knowing Jesus means knowing divine peace in a world of chaos: "Peace I leave with you; My peace I give to you. Not as the world gives do I give to you. Let not your hearts be troubled, neither let them be afraid" (John 14:27).

Contentment: Following Jesus is a life of contentment. Even in a world of unending discontentment, God grants us the ease of knowing He will provide all that we need: "For the sake of Christ, then, I am content with weaknesses, insults, hardships, persecutions, and calamities. For when I am weak, then I am strong" (2 Corinthians 12:10). The contentment that Jesus gives us is not predicated on buying the right things, crafting the right image online, or experiencing the right moments in life. This contentment is divinely given and surpasses human understanding. It is contentment in weakness, hardship, scarcity, and even death.

Unity: Although division abounds in this world—racism, terrorism, xenophobia, political discord, classism—Jesus brings deep unity into the lives of His people. God takes disparate and disconnected people and gives them eternal unity in the waters of Baptism. He draws disjointed members together and makes them members of the Body of Christ. Jesus deconstructs borders and boundaries and makes us brothers and sisters: "There is one body and one Spirit—just as you were called to the one hope that belongs to your call—one Lord, one faith, one baptism, one God and Father of all, who is over all and through all and in all" (Ephesians 4:4–6).

Heaven includes all of these elements: life, peace, contentment, and unity. The people of God, however, do not merely wait until after death to enjoy the goodness of heaven. Rather, in Christ Jesus, the reign and rule of the kingdom of heaven is an ever-present and daily reality. This is not the world's happiness. Yet, this is real happiness.

HAPPY OR JOYFUL?

The word *happy* does not occur all that much in Scripture. The word *joy*, on the other hand, is very commonly used throughout Scripture. Therefore, it seems the Bible is far more concerned with joy than with happiness.

What is the difference between being happy and being joyful? Happiness tends to be circumstantial. Sunshine, friends, and favorable conditions are all reasons for happiness. If the circumstances change, then it is very likely that one's happiness may also change. When the sun goes behind the clouds, friends move far away, or the winds blow in the opposite direction, happiness can quickly evaporate. Joy is far more resilient and steady than happiness. Ups and downs do not determine joy; rather, the source of Christian rejoicing is a deep well that cannot run dry even in the midst of hard times and struggles.

The joy of the Lord enabled Paul, while he was imprisoned (Philippians 1:7, 13, 17), to write these words: "Rejoice in the Lord always; again I will say, rejoice. . . . And the peace of God, which surpasses all understanding, will guard your hearts and your minds in Christ Jesus" (Philippians 4:4, 7). Elsewhere in Scripture, we hear a similar description of how joy transcends circumstances: "Rejoice always, pray without ceasing, give thanks in all circumstances; for this is the will of God in Christ Jesus for you" (1 Thessalonians 5:16–18). Joy is deeper and more resilient than happiness.

Does this mean that Christians are joyful but not happy? No. It is not as if the followers of Jesus unhappily grit their teeth and mutter, "We are *so* joyful." Christians are not wet blankets, buzzkills, or killjoys. In fact, having the joy of the Lord is often manifested in happiness. If anyone in this world should be smiling and singing, then it should be the people of

Jesus. Following the Lord of Life and the Prince of Peace should put a skip in our step. Being a Christian is not devoid of happiness by any stretch.

Our ultimate aim, however, it not happiness. We do not worship it, pursue it, or endlessly chase it. We have happiness; yet, the happiness we have is a by-product of the joy that comes from God. Our ultimate aim is Jesus. Dying to ourselves and living in Him gives us life, peace, contentment, and unity. As long as Jesus lives, our joy shall also live. Jesus has been victorious over suffering and despair, so we shall be joyful even in suffering and despair. Jesus has taken the teeth out of hurt and hardship because they are not the end of the story, so we will rejoice despite the hurt and hardship that abound in daily life. The Christian life is about Jesus; joy and happiness just happen to come with Him.

Cancer, miscarriages, layoffs, and even mass violence cannot diminish the joy that is ours in Christ Jesus. Evil may metastasize, dreams may never come to fruition, plans may be pink-slipped, and all kinds of violence may come our way. And yet, as sure as the Lord Jesus lives, our joy will remain. The joy of the Lord anchors our soul, buoys our spirits, and carries us safely through the rising tide of despair. How does that not put a smile on your face? (Seriously, feel free to smile right now!)

HOW CAN YOU BE HAPPY IN A WORLD OF SUFFERING?

The problem of pain and suffering is a very serious topic. *Why is there so much pain and suffering in the world? Why does God permit evil to exist? Is God lacking the power to intervene in our pain and suffering? Is God so twisted that He just sits back and watches tragedy for sport?* These questions are all part of a bigger discussion known as theodicy.

Theodicy addresses the apparent inconsistency of a good God permitting bad in the world. The most common theodicy argument goes like this: If God is all knowing, all powerful, and all good, then how is it possible for there to be evil? Either God is not all powerful and thus is unable to stop evil, or God is not all that good and actually enjoys evil. The topic of theodicy intersects with the topic of joy and happiness in a number of ways. How can we be happy in a world of suffering? Why is there reason to rejoice if so many people are in pain? And most important: where is God in the midst of pain and suffering?

One of the most well-known attempts to resolve these issues came from a German philosopher named Gottfried Leibniz (1646–1716). Leibniz put forth a theodicy that argued this must be the best of all possible worlds because God could not create anything other than the best of all possible worlds. If God is all knowing and all powerful, then He could not possibly create an imperfect world if a more perfect world was known to Him. In other words, this is the best of all possible worlds. According to Leibniz's theodicy, what appears to be bad is actually good. What we deem to be meaningless suffering actually has a place and a purpose in God's plan for all things.

Leibniz's theodicy made sense on sunny days when the birds were chirping and you were eating ice cream. (The pain of a brain freeze was just God's perfect plan for helping you to slow down and truly savor the ice cream.) However, this theodicy proposed by Leibniz broke down instantly in the midst of catastrophic pain and suffering. In 1755, an earthquake destroyed much of Lisbon, Portugal. Somewhere between 10,000 and 100,000 people died, a death toll difficult to estimate because of the limited population statistics at this time.[26] The idea that this was a good event used by God to control overpopulation was woefully wrongheaded. The French writer Voltaire used the earthquake to demonstrate the weaknesses of Leibniz's theodicy. Voltaire wrote a book entitled *Candide* (1759) roundly demonstrating the flaws in a theodicy claiming that what appears to be evil is actually good because this is the best of all possible worlds.

So how do Christians deal with issues of theodicy? Rather than coming up with our own imprudent arguments, we let God's Word speak. God did make this the best of all possible worlds; He declared it to be very good (Genesis 1:31). This best of all possible worlds, however, rebelled against its Creator and chose death over life (Genesis 3:1–8). God promised that He would do whatever it took to undo the death and destruction that came from sin (Genesis 3:15). God kept His promise—despite repeated human waywardness—over the course of thousands of years and throughout numerous generations until finally Christ arrived: "And the Word became flesh and dwelt among us, and we have seen His glory, glory as of the only Son

---

26   For more information about the death toll and economic loss incurred in the 1755 Lisbon earthquake, see Alvaro S. Pereira, "The Opportunity of a Disaster: The Economic Impact of the 1755 Lisbon Earthquake," Cherry Discussion Paper Series, https://www.york.ac.uk/media/economics/documents/cherrydiscussionpapers/0603.pdf.

from the Father, full of grace and truth" (John 1:14). God not only came in human flesh—Christ Jesus—but also He suffered pain and punishment on the cross. He allowed lies to be spoken about Him, whips to harrow His skin, nails to pierce His hands and feet, thorns to cut His brow, and His innocent life to be snuffed. Jesus died and was buried, and there He remained in the tomb. That is, until the Son of God was raised to life again: "Why do you seek the living among the dead? He is not here, but has risen" (Luke 24:5–6).

What does this have to do with theodicy? God has addressed the problem of pain and suffering in Christ Jesus. God's work of salvation did not take a detour around suffering; instead, God drove a nail right through the heart of suffering. God addressed the brokenness of sin directly. Jesus confronted suffering on the cross. He did not experience artificial anguish or pretend suffering. Jesus battled with the blood-red agony of violence, pain, and death. He stripped suffering of its power through the empty tomb. Victorious in Jesus over the eternal sting of suffering, Christianity refuses to take a detour around suffering.

In Jesus, God confronted pain and suffering. God cannot be accused of idly sitting by and watching His people suffer. Through Christ Jesus, God has engaged our pain and suffering and has firsthand knowledge of it (Hebrews 4:15). Jesus has something to say to the person suffering in the midst of chemotherapy treatments. Jesus has something to say to the child mourning the death of a parent. Jesus has something to say to the malnourished person trying to survive in a developing country. Jesus, who labored on the cross and was heavy laden with suffering, says, "Come to Me, all who labor and are heavy laden, and I will give you rest" (Matthew 11:28).

To be certain, this does not answer all our questions relating to the existence of pain and suffering. In fact, this leaves many of them unanswered. God has not revealed to us why He chose to deal with pain and suffering by taking on pain and suffering in Christ Jesus. God has not explained why He has dealt with evil the way that He has. Nevertheless, God has revealed that He has confronted pain and suffering once and for all in Christ Jesus: "Behold, the dwelling place of God is with man. He will dwell with them, and they will be His people, and God Himself will be with them as their God. He will wipe away every tear from their eyes, and death shall be no more, neither shall there be mourning, nor crying, nor pain anymore, for the former things have passed away" (Revelation 21:3–4). This promise may not answer all our theodicy questions. And yet, it answers the ones that truly matter.

CONCLUSION

Society has a fixation on happiness: We fear not having it. We love obtaining it. And we trust it will satisfy all we want or need. The Christian life often gets confused with the pursuit of happiness. Some people think that being Christian is a quick and easy way to find happiness. Some people think that being Christian means deferring happiness until heaven. Other people think that a life of happiness is found anywhere but in the Christian faith.

Clear Christianity is about Jesus. Joy and happiness just happen to come with Him. The joy and happiness we have are by-products of the life, peace, contentment, and unity that we have in Christ Jesus. These may not fully align with the world's definition of happiness. Yet Jesus defines it for us and gives us real and eternal happiness.

Clear > Confusion =
BE JOYFUL

There is a shortage of joy in our world. Which is strange. Depending on where you are reading this book right now, you are likely in one of the richest countries in the entire world. If you are living in a developed country and making an average income, then you are very likely in the upper percentage of wealthy people in the world. You likely have access to clean water and reliable shelter, and you have had enough education to read the words on this page. If you have water, shelter, and education, then you are faring better than many people around the globe.

To be certain, there are many things that make joy hard to come by: cancer, job loss, anxiety, stress, depression, family problems, and countless other woes. Still, as the followers of Jesus, we know a peace and confidence that is greater than all these struggles combined. We have eternal joy and unending happiness because of what our God has done for us in Christ Jesus. So get off the societal treadmill of joylessness and despair. Be joyful. Be hopeful. Be glad in God's love for you.

Count Your Blessings: Your grandma was right. Counting your blessings is a good practice. The sheer abundance of God's blessings makes it easy to overlook them. Carve out some time each day to reflect on the gifts and blessings that God has given to you. Write them down or post them on social media. The point of this is not boastfulness or pride; rather, the point is to recognize the many, many gifts that God has given to you. With all those blessings staring back at you, joy is bound to follow: "Bless the LORD, O my soul, and all that is within me, bless His holy name! Bless the LORD, O my soul, and forget not all His benefits, who forgives all your iniquity, who heals all your diseases, who redeems your life from the pit, who crowns you with steadfast love and mercy, who satisfies you with good so that your youth is renewed like the eagle's" (Psalm 103:1–5).

Prayer: One of the best antidotes to joylessness is prayer. Spending time in prayer pours a bucket of water on the fire of worry, anxiousness, and fear. In times of suffering and times of celebration, the people of God call on Him in prayer and praise: "Do not be anxious about anything, but in everything by prayer and supplication with thanksgiving let your requests be made known to God. And the peace of God, which surpasses all understanding, will guard your hearts and your minds in Christ Jesus" (Philippians 4:6–7).

Show Hope: Terrorism, violence, and racism used to be distant fears in faraway places. These issues are now local realities. The Gospel of Jesus Christ is hope amid hopelessness, peace in a land of chaos, and confidence despite the uncertainty of tomorrow. Hope permeates the Christian life and pierces the deep despair of this broken world. Show the world that you have hope in Jesus. This is not a vague or unanchored hope simply for hope's sake; rather, this is a sure and certain hope in the Word of God and the promises of Christ Jesus. Speak of your hope in Jesus to others. Post words of hope online. Live in a way that shows you have hope even in a world of hopelessness.

Gather with Other Christians: One of the most easily overlooked gifts that God gives us is fellow believers in Christ. These may be members of your family, people in your congregation, friends at school, or fellow Christians on Twitter. Deeper than any other connection you may have with someone else—genes, sports, politics, or food—is the connection that you have in the waters of Baptism and through faith in Christ Jesus. This is an eternal and everlasting bond that transcends age, race, socioeconomic standing, and education. The support and encouragement that we can receive from other Christians is something to be celebrated, embraced, and prioritized. Be intentional about attending worship at your local congregation every Sunday. Join a Bible study or small group. Meet for coffee with a trusted friend in Jesus to talk. Visit people from your congregation when they are in the hospital. It will not only bring them joy; it will also bring you joy:

"And they devoted themselves to the apostles' teaching and the fellowship, to the breaking of bread and the prayers" (Acts 2:42).

Christians do have the market cornered when it comes to happiness. However, it is not the sort of happiness and joy that the world would expect. The world expects happiness to be freedom to do what you want, when you want, and for whatever reason you want. The world thinks that happiness is a thing to be chased down, pursued, or purchased. Christians know that true, lasting, and eternal happiness cannot be so easily acquired. Instead, the people of Jesus know that transcendent happiness and joy is entirely the gift of God. It is a gift, however, that upends all worldly expectations: In suffering, there is hope. In death, there is life. In struggle, there is strength. In losing, there is gaining. In scarcity, there is contentment. This joy does not come from within us or by our own effort. This joy is given to us in, through, and by the grace of God in Christ Jesus.

DISCUSSION QUESTIONS

1. How is happiness the golden calf of modern society? What are some examples of this in daily life, social media, and contemporary culture?

2. What are some ways in which the deferment of death has transformed how people approach life? How have increasing life expectancy, modern medicine, and better living conditions affected spirituality?

3. In what ways is the Christian life more than just deferred happiness? How does knowing Jesus bring real and lasting happiness in the present?

4. Why does theodicy come up in a discussion about happiness? Brainstorm some possible ways you could respond to someone who states a platitude based in a wrong theodicy in the midst of suffering or pain.

POLITICAL

Aristotle described humans as being political by nature. The word *political* is built on the Greek word πόλις (*polis*) meaning "city or city-state." According to Aristotle, humans naturally organize together in communities, cities, and nations because they possess language and the desire to communicate with one another. Essentially, then, politics is just living together with other people. When people engage in political activity—dialogue, community activity, governing, legislating, voting, campaigning, protesting—according to Aristotle, they are simply doing what is natural. Politics, so says Aristotle, is only natural.

Our culture perceives Christians as being *overly* political by nature. While the ancient meaning of *political* dealt broadly with how people live together in community, modern understandings of the word have changed dramatically. Being political today means being angry, hostile, malicious, and perpetually gagging at the sight of either a donkey or an elephant (depending on your political leanings). Christians portray themselves as overly political when they live out their faith by shaking fists, painting picket signs, and hoping that religious revival will come through the voting booth. According to our culture, when Christians engage in modern political activity (e.g., throwing verbal stones at others on social media, watching only those news shows that confirm their political thinking, and seeking to legislatively impose oppression) they are merely doing what is natural. Christians, so says society, are overly political by nature.

Our culture—and far too often Christians themselves—get confused as to why the followers of Jesus might engage in politics. The confusion often comes from or communicates an erroneous belief such as, *Legislating morality will cause people to follow Jesus.* For example:

"If we can just get people to act like Christians, then perhaps they will actually become Christians. If only congress could pass a law against the use of profanity, then people would stop using four-letter words in anger and start using a five-letter word in worship (hint: J-E-S-U-S). If it were possible to get the Ten Commandments installed on every public building, then every politician and passerby would come to faith in Jesus. Passing Christian laws will make us into a nation of Christians. If we can get people to look, act, and behave in a Christian way, it is only a matter of time before they **are** Christians."

This confusion is both inside and outside of the Church. Christians and non-Christians wrongly assume that the kingdom of God rises and falls as a result of political kingdoms: votes vicariously advance the Gospel, taxes and tithing are synonymous, and political candidates do their job when they further the cause of Christ.

There is a hot mess of confusion going on here.

GOD AND POLITICS

Scripture talks a ton about politics. However, it is not in the way we might expect. The Bible is very political insofar as it does speak about the polis—how humans live together in communities, cities, and nations. There are numerous references to nations, kingdoms, and rulers. God's Word addresses how people govern and are governed, how people live peaceably in proximity to one another, and how communities are organized. In this regard, the Bible is full of politics.

However, according to the modern usage of politics, the Bible is not very political. There are no mentions of Democrats or Republicans, liberals or conservatives, the United States of America, or any other modern nation-state. There is no direct advice for exactly how to vote, whom to vote for, or whether you should post that angry political rant on social media (for the record, you probably shouldn't). The primary point of Scripture is not politics.

The Bible addresses life in the polis very differently from how the world does. The "politics" of Scripture begin with God creating all things. God created light and declared it to be good: "And God said, 'Let there be light,' and there was light. And God saw that the light was good" (Genesis 1:3–4). This pattern continued with God creating all things good: "And God saw that it was good" (Genesis 1:10, 12, 18, 21, 25). After creating light and land, water and living creatures, God looked at what He had made: "And God saw everything that He had made, and behold, it was very good. And there was evening and there was morning, the sixth day" (Genesis 1:31).

But then we hear that something was not good: "Then the LORD God said, 'It is not good that the man should be alone'" (Genesis 2:18). God made His human creatures to be in community with one another. Isolation, separation, and alienation are contrary to God's design and His intentions for humanity. Instead, He made Adam and Eve to be in proximity and community with each other. God repeatedly commissioned His creatures to "be fruitful and multiply" (Genesis 1:22, 28; 8:17; 9:1, 7). This shows God's desire for His creatures to live together in the polis and be political—that is, His desire for us to have community with one another and order in our interactions.

Yet politics and the order in our interactions in a fallen and broken world often end up being very disordered. Genesis 11 describes people coming together and creating a community. Their political ambitions were disordered and harmful: "Come, let us build ourselves a city and a tower with its top in the heavens, and let us make a name for ourselves, lest we be dispersed over the face of the whole earth" (Genesis 11:4). They desired to build a city and structure that usurped God's order and authority. They longed for a polis that could reorder their place in creation; rather than deriving their name and purpose from God, they wanted to determine their own name and purpose apart from God. This is political disorder. And it led to many other kinds of disorder: "Therefore its name was called Babel, because there the LORD confused the language of all the earth. And from there the LORD dispersed them over the face of all the earth" (Genesis 11:9).

Throughout the rest of Scripture, God addresses matters relating to politics. Most often this is in the form of general wisdom on how to live together in the polis while still having peace and community. For instance, God teaches His people how to live together by caring for one another:

"When you reap the harvest of your land, you shall not reap your field right up to its edge, neither shall you gather the gleanings after your harvest. And you shall not strip your vineyard bare, neither shall you gather the fallen grapes of your vineyard. You shall leave them for the poor and for the sojourner: I am the LORD your God" (Leviticus 19:9–10). Elsewhere in Scripture, God addresses matters that specifically have to do with how individuals in positions of power are to rule and govern well: "Now therefore, O kings, be wise; be warned, O rulers of the earth. Serve the LORD with fear, and rejoice with trembling" (Psalm 2:10–11).

The Bible describes different ways that people function in communities. But it does not prescribe exactly what kind of government or what kind of rule a society has to have. God's Word depicts instances in which kings and rulers governed effectively and instances in which kings and rulers governed ineffectively. The Bible speaks of kingdoms rising and falling, clashing and warring, uniting and dividing. It clearly has something to say about politics, government, and life together in the polis. Nevertheless, politics is far from a primary concern in Scripture.

TRUST NOT IN PRINCES, PRESIDENTS, OR POLITICS

Confusion arises when people think that politics is a primary concern in Scripture. Yes, there are frequent mentions of rulers and governments. No, that does not mean those issues are the Bible's primary concern. The Bible also mentions food and clothing with tremendous frequency; yet, nobody would argue that the Bible's primary concern is tilapia and tunics.

If anything, many of the biblical references to politics are warnings against putting too much fear, love, and trust in a certain earthly ruler, leader, or government. One of the most pointed warnings against overinflating the importance of politics is in Psalm 146:

> Put not your trust in princes, in a son of man, in whom there is no salvation. When his breath departs, he returns to the earth; on that very day his plans perish. Blessed is he whose help is the God of Jacob, whose hope is in the LORD his God, who made heaven and earth, the sea, and all that is in them, who keeps faith forever; who executes justice for the oppressed, who gives food to the hungry. (Psalm 146:3–7)

Princes perish. Rulers retire. And kings kick the bucket. God does not. He made all things, sustains all things, and rules all things. The plans of God transcend a single leader or generation. The reign and rule of God is not limited to a few short years. The equity and justice that He enacts is never term-limited, impeached, or assassinated. If there is any sort of central message about politics in Scripture, it is this: *God reigns and rules over it all.*

The followers of Jesus, therefore, are free from the anxiety and panic that characterizes modern politics. Christians do not fear, love, or trust a political party above all else. Nobody can legislate the demise of the Christian faith. Executive orders cannot rescind the salvation that we have in Christ Jesus. And there are no recalls in our eternal election as God's people. The reign and rule of God gives us a steady peace and contentment knowing that our future does not ultimately depend on earthly kingdoms.

Jesus repeatedly demonstrated this freedom from political anxiety and panic. During His earthly ministry, a number of religious leaders approached Jesus with a question: "Teacher, we know that You speak and teach rightly, and show no partiality, but truly teach the way of God. Is it lawful for us to give tribute to Caesar, or not?" (Luke 20:21–22). The question was ostensibly about paying taxes to support the government. This was a polarizing issue since the Jewish people were under the control and occupation of the Roman Empire. In reality, however, this question was a booby trap: "So they watched Him and sent spies, who pretended to be sincere, that they might catch Him in something He said, so as to deliver Him up to the authority and jurisdiction of the governor" (Luke 20:20). The answer Jesus gave to this question was stunningly simply and sharp: "'Show Me a denarius. Whose likeness and inscription does it have?' They said, 'Caesar's.' He said to them, 'Then render to Caesar the things that are Caesar's, and to God the things that are God's'" (Luke 20:24–25).

In this response, Jesus made a few things clear. First, He confirmed the legitimate existence of civil kingdoms. This is not to say that Jesus condoned the specific actions and evils of the Roman Empire. Jesus was not endorsing the reign and rule of Caesar; He was, however, confirming the legitimate existence of civil kingdoms. Jesus told them that God's people ought to give back to civil kingdoms the coins they have made. Second, Jesus' response to this question shows He was free of political anxiety and panic. We are not told in the Gospel of Luke exactly how Jesus spoke these words; however, it is not a stretch to think that He spoke them with a shrug of the shoulders

CLEARLY CHRISTIAN : CLEARING THE CONFUSION

and a smirk on His face. This question was very likely a hot-button topic for the Jewish people, a topic of heated discussion at many Jewish dinner tables and in many synagogues. This would have been a constant debate on the twenty-four-hour news channels in Judea. And how does Jesus handle it? With a simple answer that is free from anxiety or fear. His answer made it clear that His ultimate fear, love, and trust was not in Caesar.

Similar to His response with the denarius, Jesus responded to Pontius Pilate when on trial with a calmness and firmness that revealed His trust was not ultimately in earthly kingdoms or political maneuvering. After being betrayed by Judas and arrested by the religious leaders, Jesus stood before the Roman governor of Judea: "Pilate entered his headquarters again and called Jesus and said to Him, 'Are You the King of the Jews?'" (John 18:33). Jesus responded by asking Pilate whether this was a genuine question or merely something that had been supplied by the accusers. To this, Pilate responded by saying, "Am I a Jew? Your own nation and the chief priests have delivered You over to me. What have You done?" (John 18:35).

The question on hand—"Are You the King of the Jews?"—had massive implications. It had religious implications for the Jewish people since a king was the Lord's anointed. It had political implications for the Roman Empire since they ruled over the entire region. It had social implications for everyone since there was a delicate power balance between the Jewish and Roman people. And fully aware of all this, Jesus answered, "My kingdom is not of this world. If My kingdom were of this world, My servants would have been fighting, that I might not be delivered over to the Jews. But My kingdom is not from the world" (John 18:36).

Jesus makes it clear that He is a king of a different order. His kingdom is not from this world. This means, to be certain, that He is a king indeed. But the kingdom over which Jesus reigns is unlike the Roman Empire or any other kingdom in human history. And He is a king unlike any earthly king: His first throne was a food trough for animals, the only crown He received on earth was made of thorns, and His limitless power was demonstrated in weakness on the cross. Unlike earthly kingdoms where the people die to protect the king, this heavenly kingdom has a King who died to protect His people. Jesus affirms His kingship while also delineating His kingdom from any other of this world.

HEAVENLY KINGDOM
AND EARTHLY KINGDOMS

Christians recognize that they hold dual citizenship in two kingdoms. As followers of Jesus, Christians are under the reign and rule of Christ Jesus and the heavenly kingdom. As citizens of this world, Christians are under the reign and rule of the particular secular kingdom in which they live. Are Christians citizens of heaven and God's kingdom? Yes. Are Christians citizens of this world and temporal kingdoms? Yes. It is not *either-or*; it is *both-and*.

These two kingdoms are not of the same kind. There are important differences between the two. Earthly kingdoms deal with bodily justice and protection through laws and punishment; the heavenly kingdom deals with eternal grace and mercy through the forgiveness of sins. The civil realm is experienced according to the economics of home, neighborhood, workplace, and the public square; the spiritual realm is experienced according to the Word of God and the Gospel of Christ Jesus. Swords and physical strength rule the temporal estates of this world; the grace and mercy of God rule the spiritual estate of God's kingdom. These two different realms are not to be conflated or confused with one another. Nor are these two realms to be entirely separated or sequestered from one another.

Confusing these two kingdoms is very problematic. An example of this would be a judge letting a murderer go free because the perpetrator had repented of his sins. In the heavenly kingdom, this repentant murderer is completely forgiven and absolved; however, in the earthly kingdom, this convicted murderer must be subject to the laws and consequences of the temporal justice system. Another example of confusing the two kingdoms would be a Christian believing that physical force should be used to promote the Gospel. Earthly kingdoms use physical force to protect and defend citizens; the heavenly kingdom is furthered not by swords or violence but by the Word of God and the proclamation of the Gospel.

Entirely separating these two kingdoms is equally problematic. It is wrong to think that God only reigns and rules over the heavenly kingdom. God is in control of all temporal kingdoms: "He changes times and seasons; He removes kings and sets up kings" (Daniel 2:21). Earthly rulers are answerable to the One who rules over heaven and earth. It is a false dualism to think that the spiritual kingdom belongs to God and the physical kingdoms belong to the human rulers. The two kingdoms are distinct from one another, but they are not disconnected.

Christians, therefore, have a difficult task. The followers of Jesus live in two kingdoms and have dual citizenship. To be certain, it would be far easier if this were not the case. If Christians lived only in the spiritual kingdom, then they would never have to deal with the thorny issues that come with also living in the temporal kingdom. They would not have to deal with evil rulers, corrupt culture, and wickedness that are rampant in earthly kingdoms. If Christians lived only in earthly kingdoms, then they would not have to discern the activity of the spiritual kingdom in this world; they could live only by the law, go about the economic activity of the civil realm, and never have any questions about what it means to be a citizen of heaven living in an earthly kingdom. It would be much, much easier if we did not have a foot in two kingdoms.

But we do. Following Jesus while living in two kingdoms constantly requires us to discern the intersection of these two kingdoms. It is difficult when the earthly kingdoms in which we live are in direct conflict with the heavenly kingdom. It is equally difficult when it is unclear whether the earthly kingdoms in which we live are in conflict with the heavenly kingdom. What is a Christian to do when his or her earthly rulers are ruling in opposition or defiance to God? Scripture speaks to this question in a number of ways.

Acts 5

The earliest followers of Jesus boldly proclaimed the Good News of His resurrection. They had a very clear sense that they were citizens of heaven captive to the grace of God through the life, death, and resurrection of Jesus. However, living in a temporal kingdom, these followers of Jesus encountered resistance from earthly rulers. Peter and the apostles were imprisoned for proclaiming the Gospel. An angel of the Lord, however, freed them from jail, and they again began telling people about Jesus. The rulers of the temporal realm confronted them: "And when they had brought them, they set them before the council. And the high priest questioned them, saying, 'We strictly charged you not to teach in this name, yet here you have filled Jerusalem with your teaching, and you intend to bring this man's blood upon us'" (Acts 5:27–28). To this, Peter and the apostles answered, "We must obey God rather than men" (Acts 5:29). Christians are to be obedient to rulers in the earthly realm so far as that obedience does not require disobedience to God.

ROMANS 13

God appoints authorities in the temporal realm. This means that governing authorities in earthly kingdoms have been instituted by God. Therefore Paul wrote, "Let every person be subject to the governing authorities. For there is no authority except from God, and those that exist have been instituted by God. Therefore, whoever resists the authorities resists what God has appointed, and those who resist will incur judgment" (Romans 13:1–2). This is easy to accept when those governing authorities rule well and administer their duties with justice and equity. This is much harder to accept when those governing authorities are corrupt, evil, or abusive. It is important to realize that simply because God has appointed a particular authority in the temporal realm, this does not mean He condones the injustices of these leaders. God allows certain individuals to fill the role of governing authority; but God does not approve of corruption, evil, or abuses. There is a difference between *permitting* something to happen and *desiring* something to happen.

EPHESIANS 6

Being clearly Christian requires you to know your enemy. Without clearly knowing the enemy, we will inevitably wrestle with all the wrong people and all the wrong forces. And—surprise!—the enemy is not the political party that is opposite of yours. Scripture makes it clear that our enemy is not a politician, political party, voting bloc, or social movement. Rather, the enemy is Satan and the evil forces actively warring against this world: "For we do not wrestle against flesh and blood, but against the rulers, against the authorities, against the cosmic powers over this present darkness, against the spiritual forces of evil in the heavenly places" (Ephesians 6:12). Being a Christian means recognizing that there are spiritual forces of evil exerting power in and through earthly kingdoms. The earthly rulers are not the enemy; the enemy is the spiritual forces doing evil through them.

CONCLUSION

Confusion surrounding Christianity and politics is all over the place. Christians themselves are confused about how much or how little their faith in Jesus should be exercised in the public square. Non-Christians are confused as to why many people following Jesus are so political and seemingly fixated on legislating morality and trying to advance the Gospel through voting.

Christians rightfully struggle with how and when their citizenship in heaven should influence their citizenship in earthly kingdoms. Untangling the complexities of dual citizenship is no easy task. Ask anyone who is a citizen of two earthly kingdoms, and he or she will tell you about a time in which this dual citizenship presented challenges. Clear Christianity calls us to navigate life as the people of God *and* as the people of a particular nation. Our eternal identity and citizenship are in the kingdom of heaven. And yet, this does not negate our temporal identity and citizenship in an earthly kingdom. We must be vigilant as we distinguish the two kingdoms without separating them. We always confess that God is reigning and ruling over it all; we must not pretend that earthly kingdoms do not matter at all, and we must never be seduced into thinking earthly kingdoms are all that matters.

It is also vitally important for the followers of Jesus to remember that it is not the job of government—or any earthly kingdom—to proclaim the Gospel. At best, these earthly kingdoms can provide a peaceful and stable environment within which the Church can proclaim the Good News of Jesus. Passing laws to make people act in Christian ways will not bring them to saving faith in Jesus. The power of the Holy Spirit working through the announcement of the tremendous love of God in the life, death, and resurrection of Jesus does bring people to saving faith in Jesus. Throughout the generations, the kingdom of God has persisted even in the midst of hostile earthly kingdoms. Nothing—neither the gates of hell nor even the election of your political adversary—can stop the kingdom of God.

This all takes the pressure off of politics. It is hard to imagine a more tightly wound, anxiety-laden, heart-palpitating, blood-pressure-raising, just-waiting-to-explode thing than modern politics. It causes individuals and societies to freak out on so many different levels. But not the people of Jesus. We have a peace and calmness that transcends it all: Elections that go our way or the other way. Laws that we favor or laws with which we disagree. Politicians we love or politicians we'd love to see exiled to a remote island.

The people of Jesus fully engage in the life, economy, and governance of earthly kingdoms. We vote, dialogue, and get in the mix of democracy—or we are involved in the earthly kingdom in whatever way we are allowed. Still, we never panic. We know a King who is even greater. We know a Kingdom that is even better. And that King and Kingdom will last forever.

Clear > Confusion =
ACTIVE CITIZENSHIP

Be a good citizen. Vote. Run for a local office. Pay your taxes. Write your elected officials, and let your voice be heard. Engage in active citizenship. Why? Because you are a citizen.

Sometimes we try to make things too complicated. Sometimes things are complicated by nature. However, this one does not need to be very complicated. Christians are dual citizens. We have been called by the Gospel of Christ to be citizens of heaven. We have been born into a particular nation and have acquired a particular earthly citizenship. It is our duty, as citizens of an earthly kingdom, to be good neighbors by being active citizens.

A section on active citizenship may sound out of place in a book about Christianity. If so, we may have been fed a steady diet of confusion on this matter. It is completely biblical and legitimate for us to lean in and engage our earthly citizenship. Since God is active and engaged in this realm, we should be too.

Take the Time to Learn: As mentioned in the section on apologetics, take the time to learn. It is naive for us to think that we can be fully informed and active citizens if we just watch a few moments of our favorite political commentators on the television. In this present day and age, we need all our critical thinking skills to be able to cut through all the false information, biased reporting, and hidden agendas around us. Do not think for a moment that false information, biased reporting, and hidden agendas are on only one side of the political spectrum. It's on all sides—up, down, left, and right. So ask thoughtful and critical questions about the sources of your information. Check the URL and who is behind it. See what other sources are saying about this same thing. Take the time to learn.

Know Your Scope: The sheer volume of news and information that comes out on a daily basis is hard to wrap our minds around. It is impossible for any one person to learn and know all the things that are going on politically in a given country. Narrowing your active citizenship to a local or regional scope is far more tenable than trying to know all the things everywhere. Furthermore, your vocations may not give you much opportunity to directly influence matters on a national scale. For instance, a local schoolteacher or police officer does not have the same national influence as a senator or a CEO of a large corporation. This does not mean that local schoolteachers or police officers are not able to engage in active citizenship. It does mean that individuals in those vocations are in a far better position to deal with pressing local and regional matters. Do not for a moment think that local citizenship is the least important and national citizenship is the most important. National matters may receive more publicity, but local matters affect our neighbors' lives in powerful ways— sometimes even more significantly than national matters.

Do Something: After you have done the research and determined what scope suits your particular vocations, then go do something. Write your elected leaders a letter describing your desires on a particular policy matter. Attend a town hall meeting or an open forum in your state. Run for a particular office. Start a nonprofit organization to address a need in your community that nobody else is addressing. Do something other than bellyache, share articles online, and pepper the internet with angry comments.

One final comment on this matter: it is okay for us to emphasize one of our citizenships more than the other at different times, depending on the circumstances.

For instance, the apostle Paul was being tortured by a Roman tribune on account of proclaiming the Gospel. His citizenship in the kingdom of heaven had gotten him in trouble with the earthly kingdom of the Roman Empire. As he was being whipped, Paul appealed to his citizenship in the Roman Empire: "But when they had stretched him out for the whips, Paul said to the centurion who was standing by, 'Is it lawful for you to flog a man who is a Roman citizen and uncondemned?'" (Acts 22:25). In that moment, Paul chose to emphasize his citizenship in the Roman Empire.

Similarly, it is perfectly legitimate for you to write a letter to your elected leader because you are a citizen of that temporal kingdom. It is perfectly acceptable to ask questions about a municipal budget simply because you are a taxpayer of that municipality. Your Christian identity will certainly inform these interactions, but you don't have to justify your civic interactions with direct connections to how they will benefit God's kingdom. Both kingdoms that you are a part of are legitimate, and both kingdoms are under God's reign and rule. Being clearly Christian means living in the tension of having feet in two kingdoms.

1. What is meant by the statement "The Bible is full of politics"? What are examples from Scripture that show how God desires for creation to live together in community?

2. Scripture warns against putting too much fear, love, and trust in a certain earthly ruler, leader, or government. Is this a problem in our modern society? If so, what are some examples of this happening in contemporary culture?

3. What does it mean that the followers of Jesus have dual citizenship? Why is living in this dual citizenship often so difficult?

4. Acts 5 depicts followers of Jesus defying earthly rulers. Why did these followers of Jesus disobey their earthly rulers? How might this be applied in a modern context?

WINNING

Fighter pilots keep a tally of all their successful missions. Every enemy shot down, every missile launched, and every successful mission deserves another tally mark painted on the side of the aircraft. Their victories are outwardly displayed for all to see and admire.

Football players do the same thing. While not as ominous as the kill marks used by fighter pilots, football players instead use helmet stickers to mark their successes. Every fumble caused, every sack of the quarterback, and every interception is awarded with a sticker on the side of the helmet. Past prowess is flaunted on the field to intimidate the opponent.

Christians are often thought to be like fighter pilots and football players: fixated on only one thing—winning for their own glory. In a similar manner, many people perceive Christians as trying to win spiritual battles through pompous arguments, debates, and persuasion. Our culture assumes that Christians are in the game to win helmet stickers for Jesus: launching a missive from the Bible, attacking the enemy with apologetics, and then boasting about the victory with other Christians in the barracks of the church. Many in society think that winning is the goal of Christian mission.

They are sort of right. Proclaiming the Gospel is about winning. But we have to be clear about what *kind* of winning. Proclaiming the Gospel is about winning victory over death (1 Corinthians 15:57). It is about winning victory over the evil in this world (1 John 5:4). It is about winning souls for Christ (1 Corinthians 9:19–22). When the Good News of Jesus is heard and believed, there is victory over sin and Satan.

And we must always be clear about *who* is winning in evangelism. When people come to know Christ Jesus—His life, death, resurrection, and unbreakable promises—the Christian mission is being accomplished.

But when this happens, God is winning—not us. God is winning one of His precious children back from sin, death, and the devil.

The goal of Christian evangelism is not that individual Christians would win arguments or debates. It is not about proving how woefully wrong others are and making them feel like losers. Rather, Christian evangelism is about people coming to know the grace of God in Christ Jesus.

Jesus is the heart and soul, life and breath of the Christian mission. The goal is for all people to know the peace and power, love and salvation, mercy and new life that is freely given in Christ Jesus. The apostle Paul describes how knowing Jesus is the goal:

> **Indeed, I count everything as loss because of the surpassing worth of knowing Christ Jesus my Lord. For His sake I have suffered the loss of all things and count them as rubbish, in order that I may gain Christ and be found in Him, not having a righteousness of my own that comes from the law, but that which comes through faith in Christ, the righteousness from God that depends on faith— that I may know Him and the power of His resurrection, and may share His sufferings, becoming like Him in His death, that by any means possible I may attain the resurrection from the dead. . . . I press on toward the goal for the prize of the upward call of God in Christ Jesus. (Philippians 3:8–11, 14)**

That is the biblical definition of winning. It is not our victory. It is God's victory. It is God's success. It is God winning: "Not to us, O Lord, not to us, but to Your name give glory, for the sake of Your steadfast love and Your faithfulness!" (Psalm 115:1). This leaves no room for our own glory, pride, or acclaim. To God alone be the glory: "For from Him and through Him and to Him are all things. To Him be glory forever. Amen" (Romans 11:36).

Gathering glory, winning arguments, and persuading others is not part of the job description for being a missionary—nor even part of the job description of being a Christian.

SENT TO PROCLAIM ≠ SENT TO PERSUADE

God sends His people. God has been doing this from the beginning. Throughout all of Scripture, again and again, God sends His people as part of His mission of love and salvation.

GENESIS

God sent Adam and Eve out of the Garden of Eden (Genesis 3:23). Although this sending came as a result of sin, God sent them out in order to bring them back. They were not sent out to death; they were sent as part of God's redemptive work. Adam and Eve were sent so that the mission of love and salvation could occur. Similarly, God sent Abram saying, "Go from your country and your kindred and your father's house to the land that I will show you" (Genesis 12:1). God sent Joseph to Egypt as part of His lofty plans of salvation: "And God sent me before you to preserve for you a remnant on earth, and to keep alive for you many survivors" (Genesis 45:7). The first book of the Bible establishes the foundational truth that God sends people as part of His mission of love and salvation.

EXODUS

The second book of the Bible continues the pattern of God sending His people. God goes about freeing His people from captivity in Egypt by sending Moses: "Say this to the people of Israel: 'I AM has sent me to you'" (Exodus 3:14). God sent Moses to proclaim His Word and will. And after setting His people free, God sent them on a journey to be His people and enter into His Promised Land. They were sent, as part of God's grand mission of love and salvation, to live faithfully as His people and obtain the gift that God was giving them in Canaan: "Behold, I send an angel before you to guard you on the way and to bring you to the place that I have prepared" (Exodus 23:20).

PROPHETS

God did not just send a few people as part of His mission. Throughout the generations, God continually sent His people to accomplish His plans of love and salvation. This explicitly happened in and through the prophets in the Old Testament: "And I heard the voice of the Lord saying, 'Whom shall I send, and who will go for Us?' Then I said, 'Here I am! Send me'" (Isaiah 6:8). It is very important to note that when God sends His people, He also equips His people. For instance, God did not only send Isaiah, He also equipped him: "Then one of the seraphim flew to me, having in his hand a burning coal that he had taken with tongs from the altar. And he touched my mouth and said: 'Behold, this has touched your lips; your guilt is taken away, and your sin atoned for'" (Isaiah 6:6–7). Sins forgiven, lips consecrated, and guilt removed—God equips those whom He sends. Elsewhere in Scripture, God sends people to proclaim the Word of the Lord (Jeremiah 1:7; Jonah 1:2; Ezekiel 3:4–5).

The Gospels

Following the patterns established in the Old Testament, Jesus routinely sent His disciples: "And He called the twelve together and gave them power and authority over all demons and to cure diseases, and He sent them out to proclaim the kingdom of God and to heal" (Luke 9:1–2). Notice that Jesus equipped His disciples with power and authority and then He sent them out to proclaim the kingdom of God. They were not sent out unprepared or unqualified for the task; God supplied them with all that they needed for the job at hand. Jesus routinely sent His followers—not only the twelve disciples but also larger groups of His followers—out as part of His mission of love and salvation (Luke 10:1; John 17:18). As God had been doing from the very beginning, Jesus sent His followers out into the world fully equipped and enlivened with the Holy Spirit to proclaim the Good News of the Gospel.

Acts

The ministry of Jesus continued even after His resurrection and ascension. The Good News of Jesus continued in and through the ministry of the Early Church. God sent the followers of Jesus to the ends of the earth to proclaim the Gospel. Time and time again, the Holy Spirit powerfully sent people to accomplish the work and will of God: "And while Peter was pondering the vision, the Spirit said to him, 'Behold, three men are looking for you. Rise and go down and accompany them without hesitation, for I have sent them'" (Acts 10:19–20). The Acts of the Apostles is teeming with the Holy Spirit sending people to accomplish the work and will of God: "So, being sent out by the Holy Spirit, they went down to Seleucia, and from there they sailed to Cyprus" (Acts 13:4). Like a divine air traffic controller, the Holy Spirit sends, directs, and coordinates the mission of God in and through the followers of Jesus.

Epistles

As if the entire Bible had not made it clear enough, the New Testament epistles further emphasize God sending His people. God does not just send a small number of highly trained, secret-ops disciples to go and proclaim the Good News of the Gospel. He does not limit the mission of love and salvation to those with a green beret in Gospel proclamation. Instead, God sent us all into our various callings to live faithfully and proclaim boldly: "But you are a chosen race, a royal priesthood, a holy nation, a people for His own possession, that you may proclaim the excellencies of Him who called you out of darkness into His marvelous light. Once you were not a people, but now you are God's people; once you had not received mercy, but now you have received mercy" (1 Peter 2:9–10).

God has sent His people. God is sending His people. And God will continue to send His people as part of His mission of love and salvation. Being sent to proclaim the Gospel is an abundantly clear truth of God's Word. Being sent to engage in prideful persuasion, hostile arguments, and win-at-all-costs debates for our own glory is not part of God's mission.

HUMILITY > PRIDE, NARCISSISM, ARROGANCE, AND SUPERIORITY

Pride has no place in proclaiming the Gospel. Nevertheless, pride abounds in our hearts and minds. It whispers, "You are better than that person. You deserve God's grace more than she does. You have a reason to be loved by God. You found your way to Jesus." Pride is the best at telling the worst lies.

Pride, narcissism, arrogance, and superiority are words that are all too often associated with Christians. Ask some random people what words they would use to describe Christians; unfortunately, these words and others like them would probably be on the list. And consider what words may not be on the list: humble, lowly, unassuming, empathetic.

This is a problem.

Sent to proclaim the Gospel, the followers of Jesus must be ever mindful that they carry with them a gift. The gift of God's grace is unmerited, undeserved, and unwarranted. That's what makes it grace. The saccharine platitudes that pride whispers into our hearts and minds and ears distort God's gift of grace into payment for our virtue. Yet, Scripture makes it overwhelmingly clear that we are sent with a gift that has been freely given to us. And we are sent with a gift that we freely share with others.

The gift of God's grace in Christ Jesus was given to us when we did not deserve it: "And you were dead in the trespasses and sins in which you once walked, following the course of this world, following the prince of the power of the air, the spirit that is now at work in the sons of disobedience" (Ephesians 2:1–2). You were dead and undeserving of anything but God's wrath, but He called you by the power of the Holy Spirit and made you alive in Christ Jesus: "But God, being rich in mercy, because of the great love with which He loved us, even when we were dead in our trespasses, made us alive together with Christ—by grace you have been saved" (Ephesians 2:4–5). This gift of grace completely destroys any pretense of our own superiority, arrogance, or pride. God has given us the gift of grace apart from our worthiness to receive it: "For by grace you have been saved through faith. And this is not your own doing; it is the gift of God, not a result of works, so that no one may boast" (Ephesians 2:8–9).

The longer we possess this gift of grace, the more we are tempted to think we deserve it. The longer we live in the mercy of God, the more we suppose we are worthy of it. The greater we take hold of salvation, the greater our pride tries to convince us that we have a reason to boast. The truth is that God's grace is totally undeserved, we are entirely unworthy of it, and thus we have no reason to boast in ourselves.

As people sent to proclaim the Good News of Jesus Christ, it is vitally important for us to consider our demeanor and attitude toward others. We are broken people to whom God has shown tremendous grace. We are lost sheep who have been found by God. We are unworthy sinners who have been made worthy of God's presence by Christ Jesus. This means we must always keep in mind who we were before the grace of God: broken, lost, unworthy sinners who were dead in their trespasses. For those who have been plucked from the gutter of sin and death by the grace of Christ Jesus, there is no room for the following:

Pride: Reveling in accomplishments, rejoicing in acclaim, and celebrating how far we have come are all manifestations of pride. The human heart churns out pride faster than the internet churns out cat memes. And the worst part of all, pride often lays claim to the works of others. God does great things for us, through us, and despite us; however, pride is quick to claim the works of God as our own works. Following Jesus means dying to our pride: "Haughty eyes and a proud heart, the lamp of the wicked, are sin" (Proverbs 21:4).

Narcissism: This word comes to us by way of Greek mythology. Narcissus was known for his tremendous beauty. However, his fixation with his own appearance was his undoing; he became utterly obsessed with his own reflection and stared at himself until he died. While our narcissistic tendencies may not take the shape of fixating on our appearances, it is easy to become enamored with our intellect, accomplishments, morality, or even kindness. Knowing Jesus means knowing that He is the only thing beautiful and admirable within us: "Do nothing from selfish ambition or conceit, but in humility count others more significant than yourselves" (Philippians 2:3).

Arrogance: Children are great at boasting and one-upsmanship. "I can throw a rock to that fence." "Oh yeah? I can throw a rock past that fence." "Ha! I can throw a rock to the moon!" "That's nothing! I can throw the moon past the sun." Arrogance drives us to think that we are better, stronger, smarter, and all-around greater than we are in reality. The sneaky thing about arrogance and boasting is that it starts as a subtle whisper in our hearts and minds. The difference between children and (most) adults is that children think it and say it whereas adults think it and do not say it. However, our arrogant and boastful thoughts still come out in subtle statements and arrogant actions before it ever reaches our lips: "As it is, you boast in your arrogance. All such boasting is evil. So whoever knows the right thing to do and fails to do it, for him it is sin" (James 4:16–17).

Superiority: All of these—pride, narcissism, and arrogance—are manifestations of the superiority complex that plagues us all. Compensating for the brokenness and sinfulness within us, we try to justify ourselves by overestimating ourselves and underestimating others. God's Law, however, is a powerful force for flatting our superiority. We have all sinned and fallen short of God's glory (Romans 3:23). But the Gospel is a powerful force for raising us up out of the quagmire of sin. Coming to know the mercy of God in Christ Jesus means humbly admitting we deserve death but have been given life: "Likewise, you who are younger, be subject to the elders. Clothe yourselves, all of you, with humility toward one another, for 'God opposes the proud but gives grace to the humble'" (1 Peter 5:5).

The followers of Jesus have a posture of humility, graciousness, and kindness. Why? Because God alone has plucked them from the gutter of hell, washed them in the waters of Baptism, given them life in Christ Jesus, and filled them with the power of the Holy Spirit. The people of God recognize that their beauty, goodness, lovability, and intelligence have in no way contributed to their salvation. It is grace alone, through faith alone, in Christ Jesus alone.

GOOD NEWS OF CHRIST JESUS + BOLDNESS + HUMILITY = EVANGELISM

The word *evangelism* is woefully misunderstood by our culture. Evangelism connotes a wide and generally unhelpful array of ideas. These are just a few of the many, many misconceptions about evangelism:

- Evangelism must involve Gospel tracts and door-to-door solicitation. The best time to do evangelism is when people are putting a baby to bed or sitting down for dinner.

- Evangelism is wearing a t-shirt with some sort of Christian message. Extra points are awarded if the shirt has an ominous message of doom such as "Repent or Perish" or "Heaven or Hell?"

- Evangelism requires arm-twisting, proving others wrong, and outright dismissal of other people's points of view. The best evangelists talk loudly and quickly so as to inhibit the other person from responding.

- Evangelism follows a scripted flow chart of statements. Begin by saying, "_____." Allow the person to respond, and then say, "_____." If you just follow the script, then you are sure to be successful.

- Evangelism is about winning points with God. Christians do not care all that much for the person to whom they are speaking; rather, the ultimate goal of evangelism is pleasing God by persuading others to believe in Him.

Evangelism does not have to be Gospel tracts and t-shirts with ominous messages. Nor does evangelism have to be fraught with convoluted arguments and arm-twisting tactics. Rather, evangelism is as simple as speaking the Good News of Christ Jesus with boldness and humility.

SPEAKING THE GOOD NEWS OF CHRIST JESUS

The word *evangelism* is built on the Greek word εὐαγγέλιον (*euangelion*), which means "good news." This means that evangelism is inseparably combined with speaking the Good News of Christ Jesus. There is no evangelism without the name of Jesus being proclaimed. Waving at your neighbors, helping old ladies cross the road, or allowing someone to merge in a traffic jam are not examples of evangelism. To be certain, these are nice things to do. And they may even open up the opportunity for you to then do evangelism. Nevertheless, just doing nice things and loving your neighbors is not speaking the Good News of Christ Jesus. Evangelism, rightly understood, means that we are telling someone about Jesus: who He is, what He has done, or why we have hope in Him.

There is a common misconception among Christians that evangelism means telling someone *everything* about Jesus and *all* that He has done in *one single interaction*. This makes evangelism really, really daunting. It also makes evangelism sound really complicated:

> **Unbeliever:** "Oh, you're a Christian? Tell me about Jesus."
> **Christian:** "Do you have five hours, a notebook, and a whiteboard?"

There is nowhere in Scripture that suggests evangelism has to be proclaiming all of Jesus in just one conversation. In fact, there are examples in the Bible of exactly the opposite. For instance, when Paul proclaimed Jesus in Athens, a number of people asked to hear him again (Acts 17:32). Apparently, Paul had not exhausted every detail about Jesus, and people still had questions. Evangelism is proclaiming the Good News of Christ Jesus. Evangelism is not necessarily proclaiming all the Good News of Christ Jesus in one single interaction.

BOLDNESS

Being bold means being loud, forceful, and aggressive. In order to be bold, you must shake your fist in the air, post on social media in ALL CAPS, and leave a wake of destruction behind you. No. Not at all. At its core, being bold is simply being distinct and distinguishable amid everything else. This means that boldness is not necessarily big and loud; being bold can be subtle, quiet, steadfast, or unmovable. A bold font is more prominent than all the other fonts. A bold decision is distinct from all the other ordinary decisions that others are making. Boldness is simply standing out from the others when it counts.

This is why the earliest followers of Jesus were described as being bold. For example, Peter and John proclaimed the Good News of Jesus with great boldness, according to Acts 4:13. Their actions were bold because everyone else was going a different way, trusting in something else, and being satisfied with the status quo. And while everyone else was satisfied with believing that Jesus was dead and defeated, Peter and John proclaimed the bold message that Jesus was living and victorious. Paul did the same as he boldly proclaimed Jesus to the Gentiles. The bulk of Hellenists (that is, those in Greek society) were content with endlessly debating competing truths and wisdom. And Paul, with great boldness, proclaimed Jesus to be the way, the truth, and the life. Paul proclaimed the Good News of Jesus with boldness because he faithfully, steadfastly, and clearly taught how the way of Jesus is different from every other way (Acts 9:28; 14:3; 19:8).

Like Peter, John, and Paul, all followers of Jesus have been sent out with great power and authority. We do not go of our own accord or by our own authority; rather, we go out by the authority of Jesus and with the power of the Holy Spirit. This gives us tremendous boldness in evangelism. It is not by our power. It is not by our authority. It is not our message. Instead, it is by God's power and authority that we speak the message of Jesus.

HUMILITY

The boldness that we have in Christ Jesus does not negate the humility by which we live and interact with others. Scripture describes the followers of Jesus as being filled with great humility: "Have this mind among yourselves, which is yours in Christ Jesus, who, though He was in the form of God, did not count equality with God a thing to be grasped, but emptied

Himself, by taking the form of a servant, being born in the likeness of men" (Philippians 2:5–7). The reason for our humility is simple: Jesus embodied great humility. We are supposed to imitate Him. Thus, like Jesus, we, too, embody great humility.

Humility is central to evangelism. Why? Because arrogant, pompous, and snobbish people trying to share the story of a humble, lowly, and sacrificial Savior who gave His life for others sends a peculiar message. Instead, the followers of Jesus emulate their servant Savior as they live and interact with others with great humility. Oddly enough, possessing humility is one of the boldest moves in a culture drunk on pride and self-promotion.

EXCLUSIVE GOOD NEWS?

One of the more widely misunderstood and scandalous aspects of the Christian faith and the Christian mission of sharing the Gospel is the topic of exclusivity. That is, is it possible that only one particular belief system is true? Is that a claim that is in fact Christian? Is that a confusion of the Christian faith? Can other people's honestly and earnestly held beliefs and confessions offer eternal salvation?

There is a great deal of confusion around this topic largely because of the multiplicity of ways these questions are and have been answered. You have likely seen the popular "Coexist" stickers that people put on their cars and laptops. These stickers' message is rather unclear. Is this message calling for peaceful coexistence? Or by putting all the symbols together, is this claiming that all religions are essentially the same? The first message is all right from a Christian perspective; it is a good thing for people with differing ideologies to refuse to succumb to violence and hatred. The second message, calling for all religions to be viewed as essentially the same and equally salvific, is a confusion of the truth.

God's Word makes it clear that Jesus is the only way to eternal life and salvation: "And there is salvation in no one else, for there is no other name under heaven given among men by which we must be saved" (Acts 4:12). This does not leave room for claiming that there are multiple paths to salvation. The Good News of Christ Jesus does claim to be the only, exclusive good news that saves.

Think of it this way: Suppose that someone had developed a sure and certain cure for cancer. This cure for cancer was not a possible or potential cure; rather, this cure worked every single time. In order for this cure to work, the right treatments and medications had to be utilized. Deviating from these treatments and medications would not produce the cure that was intended or desired. Swapping the real medication for a placebo would result in death. Imagine what would happen if you changed the course of treatment so that instead of surgical extraction of the cancer, the revised treatment plan included using your imagination that the cancer was gone. The results would be disastrous.

The same is true for Christianity and other belief systems. God has offered a cure for sin and death. This cure is powerful and efficacious through the life, death, and resurrection of Jesus—but only through the life, death, and resurrection of Jesus. This Gospel, delivered through God's Word, is the only cure. Deviating from the cure is a disaster. It is wrong to pretend that a placebo religion will function in the same way as the real and authentic Good News of Jesus. Although the world may see this as scandalous, the followers of Jesus do not waver from the truth that the only true cure is in Christ Jesus—because God has said His Son is the only cure. But this cure is for all people.

CONCLUSION

Winning arguments and debates is not the Christian mission. Winning a contest to prove that we are smarter than nonbelievers is not the Christian mission. Winning personal glory and acclaim is not the Christian mission. Rather, knowing Christ Jesus—His life, death, resurrection, and unbreakable promises—and, with humility, wanting others to know Him is the Christian mission. Christians care about God "winning"—when He brings broken people to Himself to know His healing, love, and mercy.

God sends His people to share His love with others. The followers of Jesus have been sent to proclaim the Good News of Christ Jesus. This "sent-ness" gives Christians boldness and purpose; we are on a mission, but it is not our own mission, and we are not sent by our own authority. Rather, we go by Christ's commission with the power of the Holy Spirt in order to proclaim the Gospel. He won life and salvation for us on the cross. Therefore, we are sent by God to share this Good News of Christ Jesus not for our own victory, but so that God is victorious in His great mission of love, life, and salvation for all. Because salvation is found only in Jesus. But it is a salvation for all.

Clear > Confusion =
LOVE OTHERS

Some of the most well-known words in all of Scripture speak to the topic of love: "Love is patient and kind; love does not envy or boast; it is not arrogant or rude. It does not insist on its own way; it is not irritable or resentful; it does not rejoice at wrongdoing, but rejoices with the truth" (1 Corinthians 13:4–6).

Contrary to popular opinion, the Holy Spirit did not inspire these words so that greeting-card companies would have some nice words to put on wedding cards. Although these words are often used for weddings, these verses are not speaking narrowly about the love between a husband and wife. Rather, the love that is described in 1 Corinthians 13 is speaking to the general love that is to be shared by all people in all places.

It is a serious problem when proclaiming the Gospel of Christ Jesus is devoid of love: "If I speak in the tongues of men and of angels, but have not love, I am a noisy gong or a clanging cymbal" (1 Corinthians 13:1). The world already has enough noisy gongs and clanging cymbals (most of them are hanging out in that place called the internet). Clear Christianity is steeped in love for others. This is not the so-called "love" that our culture exudes. Christian love is sacrificial, gritty, and full of substance. A deluge of divine love flooded the earth at the birth of Jesus: "For God so loved the world, that He gave His only Son, that whoever believes in Him should not perish but have eternal life" (John 3:16). Jesus gave His life to give you life—because He loves you. The sacrificial love of Jesus has changed everything. And this love of Jesus now flows from heaven to earth into every nook and cranny of our networks and neighborhoods.

Love Enough to Care: Friends love one another enough to care. A friend goes out of her way to make sure that her companions are safe, adequately provided for, and doing well. It would be very disconcerting if a friend willfully looked away when another friend was in imminent danger. In the same way, Christians are called and commissioned by God to love others enough to care. It is not the way of love to look the other way when someone is in imminent danger of despair, waywardness, or eternal damnation. Love rejoices with the truth, and this means we are compelled to care for others both physically and spiritually. It is not loving ourselves so much that we need to prove others wrong. It is not loving ourselves so much that we use others as our conversion "successes" in order to gain points with God. Rather, it is simply loving others—loving them enough to care for their physical and spiritual well-being.

Love Enough to Listen: Sharing the Good News of Christ Jesus seems daunting if you think it depends entirely on you to say the right things. Proclamation paralysis afflicts us when we are fearful that we do not possess the right words, responses, or explanations. A large part of sharing the Good News, however, has to do with listening. Love others enough to listen to their story. Not listening to them while you organize your grocery list. Not listening to them while you look past them at the awkwardly loud guy ordering a drink at the coffee shop. Not listening to them while you scroll on to the next post on your newsfeed. Try listening to someone with undivided attention and complete focus. That is a rare gesture these days, and it is a clear act of love for someone else. This can be done in person or online. Listening to someone in person means being fully and totally present in that conversation. Listening to someone online means pausing from your other interactions, sending a personal note to that person, and finding a time to continue the conversation.

Love Enough to Talk about Jesus: Let's be totally clear—the people of Jesus talk about Jesus. If you are talking to a person who does not know Jesus, the most loving thing you can do is tell that person about Jesus. Imagine if you possessed the cure for cancer and you were talking to someone who had cancer. Would it be kind and loving to withhold that cure because it might make for a difficult conversation? Would it be a good idea to keep that news to yourself because the other person may be incredulous toward the cure? No. You would share that news in a moment. And you would be unloving if you kept that cure to yourself. In the same way, the followers of Jesus know that He has cured sin and death, brokenness and despair. We love others enough to share the news about God's great cure. Yes, it may make for a difficult conversation. Yes, others may be incredulous toward what we say. But yes, we should talk about Jesus nonetheless.

The world has more than a billion noisy gongs and clanging cymbals. Love others with the true and sincere love of God, and there will be one less noisy gong and clanging cymbal in this world. Instead, there will be one more Christian who clearly points to Jesus.

DISCUSSION QUESTIONS

1. God sends people as part of His mission of love and salvation. How long has God been sending His people as part of this mission? What are some biblical examples of this? How and where has God sent you as part of His mission?

2. Why does pride have no place in proclaiming the Gospel? What can you do to keep personal pride out of your proclaiming the Gospel?

3. The longer we possess this gift of grace, the more we are tempted to think we deserve it. How is it that living in God's mercy slowly convinces us that we somehow deserve it?

4. How can the followers of Jesus demonstrate a posture of humility, graciousness, and kindness? How can this be done individually? How can this be done collectively?

CONCLUSION

Confusion has been a fixture of this world ever since the serpent said, "Did God actually say, 'You shall not eat of any tree in the garden'?" (Genesis 3:1). In this moment, confusion jammed open a door and has dwelt among us ever since.

It took only a drop of inky confusion, a single word of falsehood, and just a bit of obfuscation. Confusion spread and spread and spread. This mingling of truth and falsehood is an aberration of God's perfect plan for creation. Compounded by time, hastened by technology, and taking up residence in human hearts and minds, confusion has afflicted us all.

Yet, Jesus is clarity overcoming confusion. Jesus is the powerful light of truth shining in the darkness. Jesus is divine peace quelling chaos. Jesus is the Word of God speaking over the noise of falsehood: "I am the light of the world. Whoever follows Me will not walk in darkness, but will have the light of life" (John 8:12). The Gospel of Jesus Christ proclaims that the thick confusion of sin has been destroyed on the cross and the radiant clarity of new life has emerged from the tomb. Confusion is dead; Jesus is alive.

The people of Jesus have always been engaged in the work of bringing clarity in the midst of confusion. This was a task given to the Early Church. This was a central effort of the people of Jesus in the Reformation. And this continues to be the work of the people of Jesus today.

We should, however, pause for a moment and consider the trajectory of confusion in this world. Jesus has destroyed the confusion of sin once and for all on the cross. And we long for the day when He returns and makes all things new. Yet, as we wait for the Last Day, we should not be surprised if the confusion in this world continues to swell and swirl with greater force. If the history of confusion in this world continues as it has for generations, then next year there will be a little more confusion than this year. The next generation will have an even harder time hacking through the jungle of misinformation and falsehood. This is a sobering thought and a sad reality.

Nevertheless, the people of Jesus are not those who succumb to despair. The joy we have because of our Lord's promises anchors our soul, buoys our spirits, and lifts us from the rising tide of despair. Followers of Jesus also refuse to be lukewarm or indifferent. We trust not in the riches of our modern technology, knowledge, or wealth. Instead, we trust in the true riches of God's truth. We daily repent and turn away from sin and confusion. We let Him clothe us in righteousness, wisdom, and life. We feast on the Word of God; we dwell in the presence of Christ Jesus; and we take hope in the comfort of the Spirit.

The only way forward to live as followers of Jesus in a world of confusion is to oppose confusion by being clearly Christian. The followers of Jesus have always been called to do this. The followers of Jesus do this today. And the followers of Jesus will continue to do this until He returns. Jesus tells us exactly what to do as we wait and hope in Him:

> **I counsel you to buy from Me gold refined by fire, so that you may be rich, and white garments so that you may clothe yourself and the shame of your nakedness may not be seen, and salve to anoint your eyes, so that you may see. Those whom I love, I reprove and discipline, so be zealous and repent. Behold, I stand at the door and knock. If anyone hears My voice and opens the door, I will come in to him and eat with him, and he with Me. The one who conquers, I will grant him to sit with Me on My throne, as I also conquered and sat down with My Father on His throne. He who has an ear, let him hear what the Spirit says to the churches. (Revelation 3:18–22)**

Confusion is dead. Jesus is alive! And He says, "Fear not, I am the first and the last, and the living one" (Revelation 1:17–18).